Bad Programming Practices 101

Become a Better Coder by Learning How (Not) to Program

Karl Beecher

Apress®

Bad Programming Practices 101: Become a Better Coder by Learning How (Not) to Program

Karl Beecher
Berlin, Germany

ISBN-13 (pbk): 978-1-4842-3410-5   ISBN-13 (electronic): 978-1-4842-3411-2
https://doi.org/10.1007/978-1-4842-3411-2

Library of Congress Control Number: 2018933065

Managing Director, Apress Media LLC: Welmoed Spahr
Acquisitions Editor: Steve Anglin
Development Editor: Matthew Moodie
Technical Reviewer: Chaim Krause
Coordinating Editor: Mark Powers

Cover designed by eStudioCalamar

Cover image designed by Freepik (www.freepik.com)

Distributed to the book trade worldwide by Springer Science+Business Media New York, 233 Spring Street, 6th Floor, New York, NY 10013. Phone 1-800-SPRINGER, fax (201) 348-4505, email orders-ny@springer-sbm.com, or visit www.springeronline.com. Apress Media, LLC is a California LLC and the sole member (owner) is Springer Science + Business Media Finance Inc (SSBM Finance Inc). SSBM Finance Inc is a **Delaware** corporation.

For information on translations, please email rights@apress.com, or visit http://www.apress.com/rights-permissions.

Apress titles may be purchased in bulk for academic, corporate, or promotional use. eBook versions and licenses are also available for most titles. For more information, reference our Print and eBook Bulk Sales web page at http://www.apress.com/bulk-sales.

Any source code or other supplementary material referenced by the author in this book is available to readers on GitHub via the book's product page, located at www.apress.com/9781484234105. For more detailed information, please visit http://www.apress.com/source-code.

Printed on acid-free paper

Dedicated to all the writers who show that serious and fun are not mutually exclusive.

Table of Contents

About the Author

Karl Beecher lives a double life as a writer and software specialist.

When being a writer, he focuses on science and technology. He likes to take meaty, complex ideas and present them in ways that are easy to understand.

As a software specialist, Karl has worked as a software engineer, earned a PhD in computer science, and co-founded a company specializing in management of large-scale IT operations.

About the Technical Reviewer

Chaim Krause presently lives in Leavenworth, Kansas, where the U.S. Army employs him as a simulation specialist. In his spare time, he likes to play PC games, and occasionally he develops his own. He has recently taken up the sport of golf to spend more time with his significant other, Ivana. Although he holds a BA in political science from the University of Chicago, Chaim is an autodidact when it comes to computers, programming, and electronics. He wrote his first computer game in BASIC on a Tandy Model I Level I and stored the program on a cassette tape. Amateur radio introduced him to electronics, while the Arduino and the Raspberry Pi provided a medium to combine computing, programming, and electronics into one hobby.

Acknowledgments

I'd like to thank my editors, Mark Powers and Steve Anglin, as well as all the others at Apress who made this book both possible and a pleasure to produce.

And, as ever, thank you to my wife, Jennifer, for her love, support, and invaluable feedback.

Introduction

So, you're a programmer, or at least a programmer-in-training.

You want to improve your programming skills. You want to become more productive as soon as possible.

You'll be working with colleagues who want their project to be successful and their code bug-free. They'll examine the code you write and serve as gatekeepers, either accepting or rejecting your contributions. Your colleagues want you to write code that's up to scratch.

The question is: how should you go about learning to do all this? One idea would be to read up on what the best programming practices are and then apply them in your work. However, the matter of how best to program is a touchy subject.

One of the easiest ways in the world to get an argument started is to ask a group of coders about good practices. Like the old jibe about economists,[1] if you ask three programmers what the best practice is on a particular topic, you'll get three different answers (and a fair few raised voices). Typical questions might be:

- Should the use of goto be allowed?

- What's the best policy for naming variables?

- What's an acceptable level of complexity for a subroutine?

- What is the maximum size for a class?

- How much code should be covered by tests?

In a perfect world, we'd have easy answers to these questions, but a world that gives us five *Pirates of the Caribbean* movies is far from perfect. The truth is that questions like these often have complex answers that depend on multiple factors. In any situation, there could be many acceptable solutions. A best practice rarely applies in all contexts.

This book helps you by taking a different approach.

---

[1] It goes something like, "Ask a question of three different economists, and you'll get four different answers."

In my experience, programmers tend to agree much more readily on matters of how *not* to program. Ask them, for example:

- Should I write code with absolutely no comments?

- Should I prefer global variables over local variables?

- If a pointer might be null, should I avoid checking its value?

To these three questions, you'd find a much stronger agreement among the answers: no, no, and *f*** no*!

Many bad programming practices exist, practices that make experienced coders grow red-faced with anger or break out in sweaty, shivering fear. The truth is, you will occasionally write code that causes reactions like this, particularly in the early stages of your career. A key to accelerating your development as a programmer will be to learn which practices are bad and then avoid them.

This book doesn't focus on how you should program. After all, competing best practices suit various projects differently. What's more, the field of programming develops constantly. New approaches are found, and existing techniques are improved all the time. A list of good practices won't remain current for very long.

Instead, this book advises you how *not* to program. It takes advantage of the fact that oodles of code has been written in the preceding decades and a lot of things have already been tried out. A combination of experience and research exists that shows which stuff works badly and is generally to be avoided.

Avoiding the bad practices listed in this book will give you a head start in becoming a better and more productive programmer. After that, you can go on to argue the issue of good practice to your heart's content.

A Note on the Style

You might have already observed that the style of this book is rather tongue-in-cheek. It gives advice as if the reader is seeking to become a failure: a programmer who ignores the rules and follows the worst practices, a programmer whose contributions are regularly rejected or (on the rare occasions they make it through review) create nasty bugs in once-functioning software. I think this makes the book a fun and enjoyable read.

Occasionally, a reasonable voice interjects and explains why programmers view a particular practice as bad. It might be because of a consensus among professional programmers or because of some empirical research. In any case, that reasonable voice appears in sections bearing the heading *Thumbs Down!*

What I Mean by *Programming*

A bad way to begin learning how to program is to mistake what *programming* actually means. Therefore, let me make clear what *I'm* using the term to mean.

After more than a decade working with software (and a misspent youth spent learning to code), I view programming as problem-solving. Roughly speaking, a programmer begins their work at some starting point, A, with a problem statement. The programmer's job is to chart a path to the goal point, B, which results in a software-based system that solves the original problem acceptably.

The journey from A to B can be long and may include many complex steps along the way. The nature of the work involved depends on how broadly you define *programming*. For the purpose of this book, I'll distinguish two types of programming:

- Programing in the *narrow sense*: By this, I refer to what many others call *coding*. Problems in this sense are problems of missing or broken software, and the solution is to write code that fixes them.

- Programming in the *wider sense*: A fuller appreciation of programming acknowledges that coding is only part of the job. The larger job is to provide a solution that is complete, high-quality, and acceptable to the user.[2] This is much more than coding. It involves other activities, like requirements analysis, system design, or acceptability testing. It also includes *lots* of communication and collaboration, not just among the programming team but with the users too. Naturally, this requires skills beyond writing good code.

This book focuses on programming in the narrow sense. That's not because the stuff involved in the wider sense is less important—far from it. I've chosen to keep the focus narrow because of who the book is aimed at. The intended audience—students,

---

[2]Sometimes called *software engineering*.

apprentices, junior developers—usually focuses on coding-related activities and should master those before they shift their attention to the wider issues.

That said, bits of stuff from the wider sense get an occasional look-in throughout the book. What's more, one of the final chapters focuses on testing, a topic that moves the discussion away from purely coding and toward coding a solution that's acceptable to the user.

Nevertheless, don't mistake this book for one that deals in wider issues of software engineering.

CHAPTER 1

Learning to Program

Objectives

In this chapter, you'll learn:

- How to mess up your approach to learning programming
- Poor ways to choose your tools

Introduction

This chapter starts things off by discussing how to learn programming and gather your tools in preparation for writing code.

Naturally, since you want to be a bad programmer, it tells you to make a mess of these tasks.

Bad Ways to Learn Programming

If you choose programming as your career, you'll probably never stop learning. Software is a fast-moving field. Radical new tools and advances come along more often than Stephen King books.

This section will show how you can scramble around trying to learn programming while taking in barely a thing.

Take a Pass on Practicing

Your Spanish teacher always told you that you'd never learn the language by reading it from a book. Practice, practice, practice, they told you. It's the only way you'll learn to speak a foreign language.

© Karl Beecher 2018
K. Beecher, *Bad Programming Practices 101*, https://doi.org/10.1007/978-1-4842-3411-2_1

But everyone knows that programming languages and spoken languages are different, right? Surely, just like math or science, you can learn programming by reading it in a book (God knows there are enough programming books). After all, you didn't learn Newtonian mechanics by building a giant centrifuge—you learned formulas from a textbook.

In short: read the programming manual but ignore the "Exercises" section.

Thumbs Down!

Actually, it turns out that learning Spanish and learning a programming language are somewhat similar, specifically in that book learning needs to be complemented by practice.

Teachers and students alike testify that practical approaches to learning programming—such as participating in quizzes, performing textbook exercises, or doing coursework—are extremely helpful when learning (Lahtinen et al., 2005). Just like foreign-language speakers, experienced programmers preach the same advice: if you want to get good, then practice!

There's just something about practical application that helps make what we learn stick with us in the long term (Dunlosky, 2013). A book can tell you what a variable is, a lecturer can show you how a `for` loop works, but to really come to grips with programming, you need to write your own programs.

Benefits include the following:

- Long-term retention of knowledge is improved, making it less likely you'll forget stuff.

- You'll habitually make fewer mistakes.

- An easier grasp of the underlying principles of programming is achieved.

Avoid Inspiration

In spite of the previous advice, you might find yourself wanting to practice your programming skills. If you don't have the self-control to resist these urges, then the question arises: what form of practice should you choose?

Whatever you do, don't waste any time being choosy or imaginative. Just grab the first exercise you can find, preferably one that deals with a topic that doesn't interest you.

I say this because when you start to think about what you'd like to build, there's a risk that you will become inspired, and inspired is a very dangerous state to be in for those intent on doing badly. It's all too easy to get swept up by enthusiasm.

Thumbs Down!

Seymour Papert, a pioneer in both computer science and education, knew the power of inspiration. One of the central principles he championed was "project before problem." This advocates letting your own interest direct your learning (Papert, 1996). Instead of being given formal problems to solve by someone else, he recommended you look inside yourself and come up with your own projects. Discover what interests you, what you would enjoy creating, and what would delight you to see built, even if just for the intrinsic pleasure of doing it. Working on something because it inspires you creatively is a powerful impulse, one that can disguise the fact that you're actually learning at all.

Be a Script Kiddie

Assuming you have a practice problem to solve, the next step is to formulate a solution, preferably a bad one.

Of course, you're not going to actually think about the problem yourself. As mentioned earlier, applying your knowledge risks increasing your retention and improving your skills.

It's far better to scour the web for snippets of code that solve the same problem. You can simply copy and paste them blindly[1] and claim that you've written a solution. You might even succeed in convincing yourself that you really learned something.

---

[1]The pejorative name for someone doing this copy-paste style of coding is *script kiddie*.

However, if you're going to take this approach, then be careful. It's not as poor a practice as you might hope. In fact, many educators will encourage you to study good examples written by others, as long as you put in the effort to understand what makes them good. So, whatever you do, don't accidentally learn how the copied solutions actually function.

Do It Alone

A good way to slow your growth as a programmer is to learn alone. If you collaborate with other learners, you leave yourself open to the following risks:

- Exposing yourself to other ideas and perspectives that can improve your own.

- Reinforcing your own understanding by explaining the material to others.

- Increasing your understanding by having material explained in terms you're more likely to understand.

- Having a greater tendency to speak up and ask questions.

- Gaining a taste of what a real team project is actually like.

Bad Ways to Choose Your Tools

Of lesser importance, but still worth consideration, is your choice of tools. This is important whether you're a beginner or a veteran programmer. There are many types of tools, just a few examples of which are featured in Table 1-1.

Table 1-1. *Examples of Programming Tools*

Type	Purpose	Examples
Programming language	Write instructions for a computer to execute	Java, Python, C++
IDE[2]	Integrates many software development tools (e.g., code editor, compiler, and debugger)	Eclipse, IntelliJ, BlueJ
Source-code generator	Automatically write programs, usually requiring the programmer to fill in certain details afterwards	A built-in feature of many IDEs, such as Eclipse and IntelliJ
GUI[3] builder	Build a graphical user interface via drag-and-drop instead of writing source code	Eclipse WindowBuilder, IntelliJ GUI Designer, Qt Creator
Version-control system	Manage the history of changes made to files in a software project	Git, Subversion, Mercurial
Code review	Submit code to be inspected and approved by colleagues	Gerrit, Review Board

Choose Inappropriately While a Beginner

We all have different levels of understanding, and so different tools can serve each of us better at any one time. As a beginner, you're still learning a lot, and learning is a balance between not being overwhelmed on the one hand and being challenged on the other.

Of course, there are obvious benefits to avoiding challenge: it's a lot less effort, and you don't learn anything new. Therefore, you should ensure that the tools you choose are overly simplistic for your current level and automate a lot of things you don't understand.

But, if you're intent on sabotaging your own learning, there are also benefits to being overwhelmed. Choosing a tool aimed at pros (like a heavy-duty IDE) might frustrate you, but be assured that you'll impress people who see you using it, and your learning progress will be reduced to a crawl.

---

[2]Integrated Development Environment
[3]Graphical user interface

Thumbs Down!

To get the balance right instead of wrong, choose tools appropriate to your abilities. If you're very early in your learning career, you might still struggle with basic concepts like variables or loops, in which case a drag-and-drop environment or a visual programming tool, like Stratch or Alice, might serve you better (Powers et al, 2006).

Once you're accustomed to a tool, you can consider exploring something more complex like Visual Basic, BlueJ, or even an IDE like IntelliJ if you're ready for it. The more complex tools tend to be more powerful.

A tool's job is usually to make a task more convenient, often by automating some things. Automation can be helpful in two scenarios:

- You don't understand a task and rely on the tool to get the task done at all.

- You do understand a task, but use the tool to get the task done quicker.

Make sure you know which of these is the case for you. For example, a code generator is all very well, but any good teacher will ask you if you understand the generated code. If not, then how do you expect to change it later if it requires adaptation? In which case, play around with the generated stuff to see how it works.

Obsess Far Too Much over Your Choices

Do you have a 48-inch TV but feel sure that a 50-inch screen would really make all the difference? Do you have an iPhone 7 but lie awake at night obsessing over the iPhone 8 and the colossal difference to your life that having one might make?

Then this piece of advice is for you: obsessing over the choice of tools as though they make a huge difference is a great way to waste time and effort. For example:

- If your project must target Java version 7, then waste hours of everyone's time arguing in favor of Java 8 because its new Streams API will somehow give you superpowers.

- If Git is your team's version-control system, stamp your feet for days on end and demand switching to Mercurial because it has magical unicorns, or something.

Thumbs Down!

The truth is that no single tool will give you an order-of-magnitude leap in productivity or quality. There is no silver bullet in software development (Brooks, 1995).

If you put forward arguments like those just given, you'll probably be outnumbered by more reasonable colleagues who'll tell you of the importance of compromising when other factors conflict with personal preferences, or that a good programmer should feel confident enough to produce good stuff using any decent tool.

Be a Fashion Victim

Hype is the plague on the house of software.

—Robert L. Glass (2002)

Don't let anyone tell you that programmers aren't vulnerable to hype.

The history of software development is littered with examples. Tool B comes along to challenge Tool A, which everyone currently uses. Tool B is 95 percent identical to Tool A, but the "hypsters" claim that Tool B is the best thing since sliced bread, so the world switches to Tool B at great cost. Next year (or should that be next *season*?), Tool C comes along and slices bread in a slightly different way, causing everyone to wet their pants in excitement all over again.

But, as the previous section explained, no single tool is going to cause huge improvements in the quality of your work. Unless your existing tool is *really* old or sucky, it's unlikely to be worth the cost of making the change.

So, if you want a poor way to choose tools, heed the hype and follow the fashions. Try to appeal to your colleagues to do the same. If you succeed, you'll spend so much time clamoring to keep up with the Joneses, there'll be little time left for real work.

CHAPTER 2

Layout and Structure

Objectives

In this chapter, you'll learn:

- How to make your code difficult to read
- Why unstructured programming helps you write worse code than structured programming does
- How to make a mess of documentation

Prerequisites

Before reading this chapter, make sure you're familiar with:

- Basic Java programming, including the following:
  - Using methods and parameters
  - `if` statements and basic looping
  - Writing simple comments and JavaDoc
- Some form of source-code editor
- The difference between source code and binary code

Introduction

The way you lay out your code has consequences for how understandable it is. This applies both to purely stylistic factors (like where to place things) and to the code's executable structure (like whether or not you use subroutines). In both cases, we'll see how to make a mess of it and render the code incomprehensible.

© Karl Beecher 2018
K. Beecher, *Bad Programming Practices 101*, https://doi.org/10.1007/978-1-4842-3411-2_2

The information offered by the layout and structure can be augmented by code comments. This chapter will also show you how to ensure your comments do more harm than good.

Make Spacing Poor and Inconsistent

Some of the most popular programming languages today are so-called free-form languages.[1] That is to say, the layout of the code makes no difference to the computer—things like the spacing between words, the number of empty lines, and the indentation. So long as your program contains no syntax errors, you can write executable code using any physical layout you want.

Of course, your colleagues will not be so accommodating. They'll expect you to follow certain rules and conventions because code that is laid out badly is harder for them to understand.

Here lies your first opportunity to cause chaos.

On the Level

Let's start with this example:

```
public class Main {
    public int number;
    public void assignIfPositive(int a) {
        if (a > 0) {
            System.out.println("a is positive");
            number = a;
        }
    }
}
```

What does the computer see? It sees that the class Main is declared first, meaning it's at the top level of the program. It also sees that the method assignIfPositive is declared between Main's opening and closing braces, which means that the method is nested inside the class. This is all a matter of syntax, which is important to the computer.

---

[1]Examples include Java, C/C++, JavaScript, and Ruby.

This is important to the programmer too, but the code's author adds additional information that the computer doesn't care about. The Main class is also considered to be at the top level by the programmer because it's declared on an unindented line. The assignIfPositive method is indented one level to show it's nested inside the Main class. The programmer also sees that the statement if (a > 0) is indented further than the declaration of assignIfPositive, which means it is a statement inside the method.

Of course, you don't *have* to indent code like this. The computer would just as easily accept the program if it looked like this:

```java
public class Main {
public int number;
public void assignIfPositive(int a) {
if (a > 0) {
System.out.println("a is positive");
number = a;
}
}
}
```

Worrying about indentation is just creating unnecessary work for yourself. After all, as soon as the code compiles, the work is done, right?

In fact, our first anti-rule helps guide us to this conclusion:[2]

Something that is not mandatory is never worth doing.

The computer would cheerfully compile this without complaint. So, why should a human complain?

Thumbs Down!

The reason your fellow programmers would complain about badly indented code is one that echoes throughout this book: source code should be treated primarily as a means for communicating with other people.

After all, the computer doesn't really understand high-level programming languages like Java or C++. It only understands the binary code that your programs get compiled into. High-level languages are just inventions that make it more convenient for humans to write and understand programs.

---

[2]An anti-rule is a piece of general advice to help turn you into a bad programmer.

Indentation makes the structure of programs more comprehensible (Van De Vanter, 2002). It acts as a visual guide for code, enabling the reader to see at a glance the individual pieces of the program and how they're related.

It also aids in the search for bugs. Look at this slightly adapted version of the previous code:

```
public class Main {
public int number;
public void assignIfPositive(int a) {
if (a > 0)
System.out.println("a is positive");
number = a;
}
}
```

See a problem? How about if I indent the code properly?

```
public class Main {
    public int number;
    public void assignIfPositive(int a) {
        if (a > 0)
            System.out.println("a is positive");
        number = a;
    }
}
```

Now the problem should be much easier to spot. In the adapted version, the `if` statement has no braces, which makes it a single-line `if` statement.[3] Therefore, the assignment to `number`—which should only happen if `a` is positive—now happens regardless of whether `a` is positive or not. This is not just a theoretical problem. Misleading indentation correlates with bug-prone software (Miara, 1983) and has also been the root cause of serious problems in real-world software (Wheeler, 2014).

Indentation is used in practically every modern software project on the planet. Your colleagues will expect it. Even most source-code editors add indentation automatically.

---

[3]With a single-line if statement, only the line immediately following the condition is considered as being "inside" the if statement.

Spaced Out

If you want to mess up the spacing of your code, a preferable alternative to indentation might be white space. This refers to the empty space between characters in source code. It can mean the spaces between tokens[4] or empty lines between blocks of code.

Like indentation, spacing makes no difference in free-form languages. The issue of white space between tokens comes partly down to legibility. However, the rules around white space tend to be looser. In code like this:

```
if(meal == "Breakfast" && hour >= 11){
    System.out.println("No breakfast after 11am.");
}
```

the condition in the if statement is pretty legible because a space exists between each token, making them more distinct.

However, white space allows for quite a bit of variation. You'll see differing styles between projects and even between individual programmers. For example, one might favor spaces between logical operators but not comparison operators:

```
if(meal=="Breakfast" && hour>=11)
```

Meanwhile, another might be very fond of spacing, going so far as to add spaces on the inside of parentheses:

```
if ( meal == "Breakfast" && hour >= 11 )
```

In any case, spacing makes the whole thing easier to read.

Yuck! Why make things easy? Try this instead:

```
if(meal=="Breakfast"&&hour>=11)
```

That's better. By removing all white space short of causing a compile error, all the tokens become squashed together, making it harder to read justlikethewordsinthis partofthesentence. (Van De Vanter, 2002). It may only make it *slightly* harder, but remember: every little bit hinders.

---

[4]A token is an individual element of program code, like a keyword, a variable, or an operator.

Tabs and Spaces

In your quest to cause chaos in your coding projects, you should bear in mind the idea of variation. It might be surprising to learn that alternating between practices arbitrarily can really mess things up.

A good example is the mixing up of tabs and spaces when adding white space. Indented code can be pushed along a line either by a series of individual spaces or by a tab character. One space pushes the line along by a single character, whereas the width of a tab character can vary depending on the editor someone is using to view the code. For example, one editor might set tab spacing to a value of 4, meaning it will push a line indented by a tab character along four spaces. Another editor might have tab spacing set to 2, so it will display tab-indented code by pushing it along two spaces.

Here comes the fun part: arbitrarily mixing up the use of tabs and spaces. In the following example, I've marked where the lines were indented by tabs or by spaces.[5]

```
public void guessTheNumber(int guess) {
••••int a = 0;
••••while (a < 10) {
••••••••a = a + 1;
  ▸    ▸    if (a == guess)
  ▸    ▸    ▸    System.out.println("You guessed right!");
••••}
}
```

That's how it would look in an editor with a tab width of 4 (which makes sense, seeing as the space-indented lines have four leading spaces). Now, see the difference it makes for someone whose editor has a tab width of 2:

```
public void guessTheNumber(int guess) {
    int a = 0;
    while (a < 10) {
        a = a + 1;
    if (a == guess)
      System.out.println("You guessed right!");
    }
}
```

---

[5]Spaces are denoted by circles, tabs by arrowheads.

The code is now potentially confusing. Your colleague may give the code only a cursory glance and believe that the `while` loop and the `if` statement occupy the same level of nesting. Or they may sense a problem, causing them to stop and expend effort trying to understand it (before going on to hunt down the fiend responsible).

Either way, being inconsistent is another nice little method for sprinkling a bit of chaos over your code. Another anti-rule for us note down is as follows:

Be inconsistent!

Thumbs Down!

Professional programmers greatly value consistency. In fact, you'll see that plenty of coding handbooks and style guides recommend something like "the exact choice of layout rules is less important than applying them *consistently*."

A project's coding standards tend to pick one option from several possibilities and mandate it. For example, Rule 5 in the Java Coding Standards of the European Space Agency says, "Do not use tab characters in implementation files, use plain spaces instead" (ESA, 2004).

Modern editors and IDEs even come with built-in functionality for enforcing spacing and indentation rules. These programs can format your code automatically, structuring the code layout in specific ways. Some code-review tools can even be made to automatically reject submissions that don't adhere to standards.

Clutter the Code

Perfection is achieved not when there is nothing more to add, but when there is nothing left to take away.

—Antoine de Saint Exupéry (1939)

Programming is hard, even for experienced veterans. It requires the management of great complexity and the ability to hold a lot of constantly changing information in one's head all at once.

Naturally, this requires a great deal of concentration. Anything that distracts or confuses the programmer threatens to break that concentration, and a programmer who cannot concentrate risks making mistakes. You could distract your colleagues while they're trying to work by playing loud music or by gently yet persistently prodding the side of their head with a stick. But there's no need to be so overt. The good news is that you can actually distract them just by writing code!

Programmers like clean, uncluttered code. Cluttered code has a lot of extra crap that doesn't need to be there, which is very distracting to a programmer who is trying to concentrate.

Unused Stuff

Distract those reading your code by declaring things but then never using them. For example, a reasonable person expects that a declared variable will be used at some point, so seeing unreferenced variables trips them up. Consider this:

```
public double applySecretFormula(
        int a, int b, int c, int d) {
    return (a^2 / (b + 1)) * c;
}
```

The function references three variables (a, b, and c), but the list of parameters includes a fourth: d. Now, anyone looking at this code is going to be stopped in their tracks. What's d doing there? Is it a mistake in the parameter list? Or is the secret formula incomplete? Or did it used to include d in the past but now no longer uses it, meaning someone forgot to remove it from the parameter list? The code doesn't readily reveal the answer.

Dead Stuff

Another form of clutter is unreachable code, also known as dead code. This is code that is actually impossible to reach under any circumstances. Since it serves no purpose, unreachable code merely wastes space, both in the computer's memory and the reader's brain.

It can be recognized quite easily in some forms; for example:

```
public int applyDiscount(int quantity) {
    if (quantity > 10) {
        return price - 10;
    }
    else {
        return price;
    }
    System.out.println("Discount checked!");
}
```

In this case, there is no way to reach the `println` statement, because every possible path through the method ends up at a return statement before the `println` can be reached. But this would be an easy example to catch. Code-analysis tools could pick it up, and, in the case of Java, the compiler would treat this as a compile-time error.

If you want to introduce unreachable code, you should do so in a much more subtle and harder to detect fashion; for example:

```
public void doProcessRandomly() {
    double n = Math.random();

    if (n > 10) {
        // All code inside the if-block is dead
    }
}
```

Can you see the problem here? The compiler certainly can't. As far as the compiler is concerned, the built-in method `Math.random` returns a `double` value. However, what the compiler doesn't know and cannot work out is that `Math.random` is written in such a way that it will only ever return a number between 0 and 1. No matter how many times you run the code, n will *never* exceed 10, thus none of the code inside the `if` block is reachable because n must exceed 10 before the code in the `if` block gets executed.

Disabled Stuff

Being told to remove code from a program might make you nervous. You might have grown attached to that bit of code. Or you might fear forgetting all about it after deletion. What if it needs to be put back again in the future?

Can't you just take it out, but at the same time leave it in?

Sure you can! Just turn the code into comments and hope that your project is not one of those that prohibits this practice.

Thumbs Down!

In all these cases, the advice from your colleagues will usually be the same: if it's useless, remove it. Any code that contributes nothing to the execution of a program is seen as wasteful clutter or, even worse, a potential bug. Programs with unnecessary code in them correlate with higher rates of defects (Card et al., 1986).

Don't worry too much about accidentally deleting something that turns out to be useful. You can always rescue it from a previous version stored in your version-control system.

You do use version control, don't you?

Write Bad Comments

Things like layout, spacing, and clutter contribute to the comprehensibility of your code. They're also fairly systematic, so much so that automated tools can enforce rules around them.

Comments also affect how well your code can be understood. However, writing them is a much more creative endeavor. Automated tools can't write them for you or, more important, tell you when they're done badly.

This makes them potentially dangerous. Write them well, and the reader's understanding is improved. Write them badly, and the reader will be confused, misled, and greatly annoyed.

I think you know where this is leading.

No Comment!

The least labor-intensive way of writing bad comments is to not write them at all. As the old anti-wisdom says,

If it was hard to write, then it should be hard to read.

If you want to make trouble, writing code without comments should be the first thing to try. When you submit your code, leave out any explanation of how it works. You never know—you might get away with it!

Thumbs Down!

The point of a comment is to clarify the code. But if your code does something very simple and obvious, a comment is probably unnecessary. Leaving out the comments on a piece of code like this will be fine:

```
public void getWeight() {
    return weight;
}
```

After all, everyone knows what a getter method is.

However, code like the following is not at all obvious:[6]

```
for (i = 0; i < numbers.length; i++) {
    for (int j = 1; j < (numbers.length - i); j++) {
        if (numbers[j - 1] > numbers[j]) {
            Integer temp = numbers[j - 1];
            numbers[j - 1] = numbers[j];
            numbers[j] = temp;
        }
    }
}
```

In this case, comments would clarify its purpose greatly. If your code looks complicated (and it should be, if you're following the advice in this book!), you're unlikely to get away with leaving out the comments.

You can suck a lot of the fat out of the process of writing comments by using tools to help you. For example, comment generators can read the code and set up some skeletal comments for you. Your job is then to fine-tune what the generator produces.[7] Another useful tool is a documentation generator. This extracts information from the code—including but not limited to the comments—and uses it to generate documents describing the code, typically in HTML or PDF format.[8]

Code Parroting

So, your attempt to sneak through some commentless code failed? Never fear. There is still plenty of scope to do it wrong.

The next worst thing to writing no comments is to simply write comments that parrot the code. For example, if your colleagues respond to the preceding example with a comment like "Needs more comments!" then fine—give 'em what they want.

---

[6]For your interest, this piece of code implements a Bubble Sort.

[7]An example of a comment generator is Atomineer (`www.atomineerutils.com/`).

[8]Examples include Doxygen (`doxygen.org`) and Javadoc, which comes built into the Java programming environment.

Here are some comments explaining what's happening inside the if block:

```
if (numbers[j - 1] > numbers[j]) {
    // numbers[j - 1] is assigned to temp
    Integer temp = numbers[j - 1];
    // numbers[j] is assigned to numbers[j - 1]
    numbers[j - 1] = numbers[j];
    // temp is assigned to numbers[j]
    numbers[j] = temp;
}
```

Do you see how wonderfully useless the comments are? Notice how they add no semantic information to the code whatsoever? Comments like this reach an admirable level of unhelpfulness.

Thumbs Down!

Good comments clarify the code and explain the meaning behind it. They *add* information. The comments in the previous example didn't do that. They simply stated what each step did without giving any context.

Individual steps are typically not what the reader is concerned about (a programmer knows an assignment when they see one). What normally troubles them is knowing what *groups* of operations are doing and what goal they're all working together to achieve. Useful comments are ones explaining at this level (Shneidermann, 1979).

A more useful way to comment the previous example might be as follows:

```
// Compare the values of two consecutive numbers.
// Swap their positions in the numbers array if
// the earlier is greater than the latter.
if (numbers[j - 1] > numbers[j]) {
    Integer temp = numbers[j - 1];
    numbers[j - 1] = numbers[j];
    numbers[j] = temp;
}
```

So would a summary explanation of the whole routine:

```
// Sorts the values in the numbers array into
// ascending numerical order using a bubble
// sort algorithm.
for (int i = 0; i < numbers.length - 1; i++) {
    for (int j = 1; j < (numbers.length - i); j++) {
        // etc...
```

Out of Sync

So, you tried to write commentless code, but they caught you. Then, you tried to be facetious and add useless comments, but even that was rejected. Have they got you pinned down now? Is there no other way to use comments badly?

Actually, there is something else, perhaps the most evil possibility of them all. Think of it this way: a comment is supposed to explain a piece of code, but what if the explanation in the comment doesn't match the behavior of the code? This inconsistency indicates one of two potential problems: 1) the code is incorrect, or 2) the comment is incorrect (Tan, 2012).

This is a nicely messy situation to introduce; first, because you now have two possible problems to consider (and don't forget, both could be true!). And second, because it would be easy to sneak the inconsistency into the codebase.

Look at this example:

```
/**
@param message The message to be displayed. If null,
    an empty message is displayed.
*/
public void displayMessage(String message)
{
    if (null == message) {
        message = ""
    }
    System.out.println(message);
}
```

Good so far. Now, let's say the method functionality is changed at a later point, specifically so that a null `message` parameter will no longer print an empty message. However, the comment is left untouched.

```
/**
@param message The message to be displayed. If null,
    an empty message is displayed.
*/
public void displayMessage(String message)
{
    if (null == message) {
        return;
    }
    System.out.println(message);
}
```

Regrettably (for everyone else at least), it's all too easy to miss that the comment and the code now no longer match. In review, your colleague may well concentrate on what *has* changed, but overlook what *hasn't* changed. The `displayMessage` method now no longer works with null values, but anyone relying on the comments when using the method will be misled.

Even good programmers, who earnestly try to write programs well, can easily make this kind of mistake.

Avoid Structured Programming

Layout describes the appearance of your code, aspects of which make little or no difference in the way a program is executed (use of tabs, placement of tokens, amount of whitespace, and so on). *Structure* describes how the executable parts of your program are arranged. Like the layout, you get to choose your program's structure, and it can end up clear or convoluted.

Before we get to the next lesson, a quick bit of history. In the elder days of programming (1970s and earlier), many languages were unstructured. Controlling the flow of execution through an unstructured program was achieved using very simple `if` statements and unconditional jumps (a.k.a. `goto` statements). Individual statements had labels or line numbers. A `goto` statement would immediately transfer control to the referenced statement.

If you ever read *Choose Your Own Adventure* books, they work along similar lines ("If you stay to fight the goblin, go to page 231. If you decide to flee, go to page 193").

For example, consider this program written in an old language called BASIC.[9] It goes through the numbers 1 to 10 and prints out whether each one is odd or even.[10]

```
10 let x = 1
20 if x > 10 then goto 90
30 if x mod 2 = 0 then goto 60
40 print x, " is odd"
50 goto 70
60 print x, " is even"
70 let x = x + 1
80 goto 20
90 print "Finished"
```

You can picture the flow of control through this program by drawing a simple flow-control diagram, like in Figure 2-1.

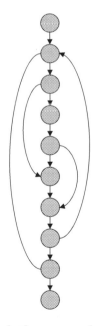

Figure 2-1. *Flow of control through the example BASIC program*

---

[9]Beginner's All-Purpose Symbolic Instruction Code, a programming language invented in 1964 (Kemeny and Kurtz, 1964).

[10]The mod operator is short for modulo. It calculates the remainder of a division. If dividing *x* by 2 results in a zero remainder, then *x* is an even number.

In the diagram, each node represents a statement, and the arrows show the flow of control between those statements. This is a very small program, but already the flow of control is getting complicated. Its structure is ad-hoc, and there are lots of potential pathways from the beginning to the end of the program.

Larger unstructured programs consisting of thousands of statements tended to have so many goto statements that they became known as spaghetti code, since the lines on their control-flow diagrams ended up resembling a hellish tangle of spaghetti strands.

Structured programming emerged in reaction to the unbridled use of goto statements (Dijkstra, 1968). It argued that all programs could (and should) be written using only a small set of standard structures, like sequences, decisions, and loops. Those structures are modeled in Figure 2-2. An individual node in these diagrams can represent not just individual instructions, but whole collections of statements (i.e., blocks).

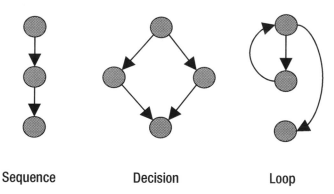

Sequence   Decision   Loop

Figure 2-2. *Fundamental programming structures*

In a language like Java, these structures are available as things like if statements and for loops. The earlier unstructured program could be rewritten without gotos in a structured language like Java, as follows:

```java
for (int x = 1; x <= 10; x++) {
    if (x % 2 == 0) {
        System.out.println(x + " is even");
    }
    else {
        System.out.println(x + " is odd");
    }
}
```

Its resulting flow-control diagram (Figure 2-3) is simpler because fewer independent paths exist through the code.

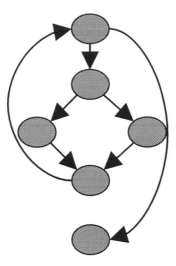

Figure 2-3. *Control-flow diagram of the Java program*

Jump Around

After this history lesson, you might be eyeing the goto statement keenly, your mouth watering at the mess you could make with it. To hell with the structured stuff, you might think.

But hold your horses! Unstructured programming has been largely banished from the programming world. Structured programming has been entrenching itself since at least the 1960s. Fighting against it is therefore going to be hard.

Under normal circumstances, my first piece of anti-advice would be to use goto statements as much as you can. However, goto occupies a special place in the programming hall of infamy, generally despised and regarded as a touchstone of bad programming practice. Many coding standards forbid its use entirely (for example, see National Weather Service, 2007; JPL, 2009) or strongly recommend against it.

Consequently, any attempt to use goto these days is likely to be crushed swiftly. In fact, some of today's most popular languages (like Java and Python) don't even include a goto statement, their designers having been mindful of its reputation. Even projects that allow goto statements tend to use it only in strictly-defined scenarios (see for example, kernel.org, 2017).

In this case, I will therefore make an exception and recommend that you don't bother trying to use goto instructions, because it's probably a waste of your time. Instead, I recommend you try to work within the bounds of structured programming and abuse its fundamental structures. This book has whole chapters dedicated each of them. To learn how to be dastardly with decisions, read Chapter 4. To see how you can make your colleagues loopy with loops, read Chapter 5. Subroutines, which are also discussed briefly in the next section, get a more complete treatment in Chapter 6.

Routine Work

Another fundamental structure in structured programming is the subroutine. This is a unit of code you can call on to perform a task. They are available in several forms, including procedures, functions and—in the case of an object-oriented language like Java—methods.

If you don't organize your code into subroutines, then your program ends up as a huge wall of text. This fits nicely with one of the anti-rules of programming:

In general, bigger is better.

"Bigger is better." That feels so emotionally satisfying, there's just no need to even question it. Let's see the earlier example of the bubble-sort code incorporated into a larger program that dispenses with subroutines:

```
Integer[] numbers = new Integer[5];
Scanner keyboard = new Scanner(System.in);
System.out.print("Enter filename> ");
String filename = keyboard.nextLine();
filename = filename.concat(".txt");
File inputFile = new File(filename);
BufferedReader reader = new BufferedReader(new FileReader(inputFile));
String text = null;
int i = 0;
while ((text = reader.readLine()) != null && i < 5) {
    numbers[i] = Integer.parseInt(text);
    i++;
}
reader.close();
```

```java
for (i = 0; i < numbers.length; i++) {
    for (int j = 1; j < (numbers.length - i); j++) {
        if (numbers[j - 1] > numbers[j]) {
            Integer temp = numbers[j - 1];
            numbers[j - 1] = numbers[j];
            numbers[j] = temp;
        }
    }
}
for (i = 0; i < numbers.length; i++) {
    System.out.println(numbers[i]);
}
```

This wall of text . . . pardon me . . . this *piece of code* carries out at least four extra tasks in addition to sorting numbers.[11] Understanding them requires a reader to go through the code line by line. This imposes a burden on the reader that is unnecessarily time-consuming and laborious if they're not focusing on the details. And, being only about twenty lines long, this is considered a very small program. The problem only intensifies with longer ones.

Thumbs Down!

You can describe what a piece of code does at many levels.

At a lower level (closer to the details), you can describe what single statements do or see how the state of individual variables gets changed.

At a higher level (further away from the details), you can describe the code in terms of its purpose. The higher-level view describes code conceptually rather than in terms of the nitty-gritty.

Consider the bubble-sort code. At the lower level, you can talk about how this code maintains two indexes, i and j, each of which serves as a pointer to a specific value in the array numbers. You can explain how one for loop iterates i over the complete length of numbers one value at a time, etc. At a higher level, you can clump groups of statements together and refer to them as a whole (without reference to variables and if statements and loops and so on). Then, you could say that the code sorts an array of integers into ascending numerical order by performing a bubble sort on them.

---

[11]It also contains several bonus bad practices that you might recognize after reading subsequent chapters.

Programmers like to be able to move easily between high levels and low levels as required. They might begin at the high level, considering only *what* a program is trying to do without being distracted by lower-level details. Subsequently, they might need to drill down to an interesting bit of the code to see *how* it works in lower-level detail (for example, to look for a bug in the code or to optimize it).

Subroutines give programmers that flexibility. Failing to put your code into subroutines grounds everyone at the lower level among the grubby, nitty-gritty details and denies them the option of viewing things at higher levels.

Large, monolithic programs like the last example can be rewritten to use subroutines. Rewriting the previous example would involve:

- Creating several new subroutines

- Moving the relevant portions of code into each subroutine

- Writing a chain of subroutine calls

Perhaps like this:

```
Integer[] numbers = new Integer[5];
String filename = askUserForFilename();
File inputFile = openFile(filename);
readNumbersIntoArray(inputFile, numbers);
bubbleSort(numbers);
outputNumbers(numbers);

// ...

public String askUserForFilename()
{
    Scanner keyboard = new Scanner(System.in);
    System.out.print("Enter filename> ");
    String filename = keyboard.nextLine();
    filename = filename.concat(".txt");
    return filename;
}

// etc.
```

Now, it's much easier to see at a glance what the program does.

Another important reason to use subroutines is to prevent the same code from being written twice. Programmers particularly hate code duplication. To see why, imagine that the last example were amended so that the code outputs the array of numbers twice: once before sorting and once after.

- *Without* using subroutines, you'd have to write the code for outputting the array contents again at an earlier stage in the code.

- *With* a subroutine, you'd need only add an extra call to the `outputNumbers` method.

Of course, that doesn't save a huge amount of extra effort, but that's not where the payoff comes. The payoff comes later when a change becomes necessary to the way the array contents are output. If the code responsible is in a subroutine, you only need to change it in one place. If, on the other hand, the code responsible is duplicated, you'd have to update all those copies, ensuring that each change is done exactly the same and that *none* of those copies is missed accidentally. You can well imagine this gets harder the more the code is duplicated and the more those duplicates are spread out.

This is the motivation behind another anti-rule for the bad programmer:

Duplicate! Spread stuff around; don't consolidate things.

Subroutines will be discussed in more detail in Chapter 6.

CHAPTER 3

Variables

Objectives

In this chapter, you'll learn:

- The chaos that poorly named variables can induce
- How to do variable declaration in a confusing way
- Why being lax with the scope of variables causes problems
- How to abuse the type system of a language
- The power of null to cause trouble

Prerequisites

Before reading this chapter, make sure you're familiar with basic types, like integers, strings, and collections.

Introduction

Where would programmers be without variables? Without them, there would be no way to record and keep track of information as a program goes about its business.

As variables are such a fundamental feature of programming, it should delight you to know that there exist numerous easy ways to misuse them. This chapter will cover some of the most notorious and readily visible bad practices.

© Karl Beecher 2018
K. Beecher, *Bad Programming Practices 101*, https://doi.org/10.1007/978-1-4842-3411-2_3

Use Obscure Names—Thinking Up Meaningful Labels Isn't Worth the Effort

There are only Three hard problems in Computer Science: cache invalidation, naming things, and off-by-one errors.

— Phil Karlton (Source: The Internets)

The preceding quote, one that's widely appreciated among programmers, should fill you with a wonderful feeling of foreboding. If software folk find it so hard to name things, getting it wrong should be easy.

All Meaningless

In most programming languages, variable names can typically reach whatever length the programmer desires. But why waste your time typing long names into the editor?

Think about it: a variable called `amount` has six letters in its name. If you refer to that variable twenty times throughout a program, that's 120 keystrokes right there. However, if you shorten the name instead to `a`, that's five keystrokes saved every time, adding up to a reduction of one hundred keystrokes.

Just think of what you could do with the time saved!

In fact, why risk incorporating even the merest hint of meaning in your variable names? A colleague with their wits about them might guess that `a` means *amount*. Instead, just use an arbitrary letter. You've got 25 others to choose from.

The beauty of this "strategy" is that it has no natural limit. Exhausted all 26 letters of the alphabet? Just add a second character, yielding names like `aa` and `x1`.

Thumbs Down!

In this day and age, when many IDEs provide auto-completion, there's no excuse for shortening variable names. Reviewers will complain that names should carry meaning so that readers of your code don't have to continually look up what a variable actually refers to. Instead, with meaningful names, they can concentrate on what your code is doing.

Consider this example:

```
int a = 10000;
Map<String, Double> p = new HashMap<>();
```

```
for (int i = 0; i < 193; i++) {
    int q = getCountryPopulation(i);
    int b = getCountryArea(i);
    String n = getCountryName(i);

    if (q > a) {
        double r = q / b;
        p.put(n, r);
    }
}
```

This snippet of code calculates the population densities of countries greater than 10,000 square kilometers in size and puts those values into a map. It would be much easier to understand with clearer variable names:

```
final int minimumArea = 10000;
Map<String, Double> populationDensities =
        new HashMap<>();

for (int i = 0; i < 193; i++) {
    int population = getCountryPopulation(i);
    int area = getCountryArea(i);
    String name = getCountryName(i);

    if (population > minimumArea) {
        double populationDensity = population / area;
        populationDensities.put(name,
                populationDensity);
    }
}
```

Your reviewer might make exceptions for some names in a few circumstances. For example, index variables in short loops are usually allowed to be named something like i or n. They'll advise you to "be guided by your common sense" or something similarly dangerous.

As a bonus practice, notice that the minimumArea variable has become a constant instead of a variable (thanks to the final keyword). You'll be encouraged to mark as constant any values that shouldn't change throughout the program so as to guard against their being updated accidentally.

Vowel Movements

Using one-letter variable names will likely result in your code's being sent back fast with a message like "use more descriptive names please!" But this doesn't mean your quest to use awful variable names ends here.

Another technique — one that allows you to both obfuscate names and get right up the reviewer's nose at the same time—is to remove all the non-leading vowels from a name. See the wonderful effects in these examples:

- `velocity` becomes `vlcty`

- `volume` becomes `vlm`

- `count` becomes `cnt`

- `price` becomes `prc`

- `quantity` becomes `qntty`

- `total` becomes `ttl`

Notice how the shortened versions sort of, kind of look like the original names? They bear enough resemblance to let you argue they're meaningful, but they're still likely to cause the reviewer headaches from having to continually check and recheck the meaning. The best thing about this technique is it allows you to be pedantic. The reviewer wanted you to use longer names, and so you have!

Thumbs Down!

Good programmers aren't above using shortened names themselves. Certain style guides will tell you things like:

- If you must abbreviate, limit it to local variables used in a single context (GNU, 2016).

- Shorten words, don't delete letters within a word (Google, 2017a).

- Use commonly-accepted abbreviations, like `num` or `url`, and use them consistently; don't switch between the full name and shortened version throughout the code (Apple, 2013).

Lazy Naming

Programmers are problem solvers. If naming variables is a hard problem, then the solution is obvious: spend less effort on doing it. This way, you get lousy names and have expended barely any effort in the process. Problem solved. But which labor-saving techniques are available?

One of my favorites is to name a variable after its type. Just look how impressively useless these names are:

```
String string;
int number;
boolean flag;
```

Now, imagine the reviewer looking at the names. "Number of what?" they scream. Or, "Of course it's a flag, it's a Boolean, but *what* is it flagging?"

Ah, warms your heart, doesn't it?

Another form of uselessness is ambiguity in names. There's nothing more infuriating than an integer variable called count ("A count of *what*?") or a subroutine called doProcess ("Aagggghhh!").

Treat Variable Declaration Like a Waste of Time

Statically typed languages like Java require you to declare variables before using them. The whole business of declaring and initializing variables is typically governed by clear rules in almost every coding standard and textbook.

But who's got time for that? Here's how to do declarations the quick and dirty way.

Be Confusing

You might not have realized how much variable declarations can be fertile ground for sowing confusion. After all, they seem so simple and innocent.

In fact, just doing something like declaring multiple variables on one line can cause confusion. Check this out:

```
int scoreBob, scoreJohn = 10;
```

After executing this statement, both Bob and John got a score of 10, right? Wrong. John got 10, because his variable was declared *and initialized*, but Bob's variable was only declared. An uninitialized `int` in Java means that variable has a value of 0. In this case, poor old Bob ends up with no score.

Thumbs Down!

You'll find some anal-level attention to detail in some coding standards and textbooks when it comes to variable declaration. For example, most of them don't leave to chance the question of whether declarations should be one-per-line or not (Long, 2013). The answer, apparently, is almost always that they should.

```
int scoreBob = 10;
int scoreJohn = 10;
```

Be Contrarian

Sometimes there's no generally agreed-upon rule on an issue. One project likes method A, another likes method B. This can cause a dilemma for a coding chaos monkey. How do you break a rule when the rule varies?

Simple: Be contrarian. Check which rule *your* project prefers and do it differently. Remember the earlier anti-rule: *Be inconsistent*.

Variable declarations are a good example of this. Standards differ on whether a variable's initialization and declaration should be done together and close to its first use. Oracle's Java code conventions, for example, advise that all declarations be done at the beginning of a code block and that initializations be done later (Oracle, 1999). On the other hand, Google's Java guidelines require that declaration happens together with initialization as close as possible to the variable's first use (Google, 2017b).

Based on my personal experience, I'd say people generally prefer the latter approach, and several prominent textbooks agree (for example, Martin, 2009; McConnell, 2004).

So, if your project prefers the latter approach too, then separate out your declarations and initializations. Try putting the declaration of the variable near the top of a routine, the initialization somewhere in the middle (preferably in among some lines of code that don't actually reference that variable), and finally tuck the first actual use of the variable even further down.

Here's what might go through the mind of someone reading code written like that:

- Upon first seeing the declaration (int foo) they'll think, "OK, this routine contains an integer called foo."

- Then, as they read on, they'll get caught up in other details.

- Later, they'll encounter the initialization of foo. "Oh, this must be where foo is used. I'd forgotten about that."

- At this point, they'll get distracted and frustrated, as no reference to foo is actually made in the immediate vicinity. They might even lose their grip on what the wider routine is really doing and get delightfully pissed off.

Maximize the Scope of Variables

The scope of a variable tells you which parts of a program have access to it. A narrow scope means the variable can only be accessed by a small part of the code. A wide scope means it can be accessed by most, if not all, of the program.

This section will help show you the wonderfully terrible consequences of giving your variables as wide a scope as possible.

Broad Scopes

For a long time now, programming literature has recommended narrowing the scope of your variables as much as possible. But why cramp your own style? You never know which parts of a program might need access to a variable in the future, so why not allow a variable to be accessible by *all* parts?

Consider this example, a partial view of a class that draws basic shapes:

```java
import com.acme.drawing.Renderer;

public class Shapes {
    public String color = "white";
    public Point center;
    public int radius;
```

```
    public void drawCircle() {
        Renderer.drawCircle(center, radius, color);
    }
}
```

The variables color, center, and radius are fields of the Shapes class, which means they have a relatively wide scope. As soon as you create an instance of Shapes, they exist, and all methods in Shapes can access them.

Here's some code that uses Shapes to try to draw a pair of eyes with white corneas and black pupils.

```
public void drawEyes() {
    Shapes shapes = new Shapes();

    // Draw left eye
    shapes.center = new Point(50, 50);
    shapes.radius = 20;
    shapes.drawCircle();

    // Draw left pupil
    shapes.color = "black";
    shapes.center = new Point(50, 50);
    shapes.radius = 10;
    shapes.drawCircle();

    // Draw right eye
    shapes.center = new Point(100, 50);
    shapes.radius = 20;
    shapes.drawCircle();

    // Draw right pupil
    shapes.color = "black";
    shapes.center = new Point(100, 50);
    shapes.radius = 10;
    shapes.drawCircle();
}
```

Looks good, right? Anyone looking at the code not too carefully would expect the eyes to appear as they do in Figure 3-1. However, because the code actually smuggles in a bug, the resulting image actually looks like Figure 3-2.

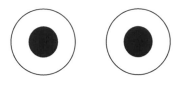

Figure 3-1. *Big eyes*

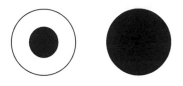

Figure 3-2. *Bug eyes*

Thumbs Down!

The problem with the preceding example is that, after drawing the left pupil, the color property remains black and isn't changed back to white before the second eye is drawn.

This illustrates a central cause of headaches when using variables with excessive scope: the need to carefully manage state. By expanding the scope of variables, you force the programmer to juggle more details, increasing the chance that mistakes are made.

The Shapes example could be rewritten like this:

```
public class Shapes {
    public void drawCircle(Point center, int radius,
            String color) {
        Renderer.drawCircle(center, radius, color);
    }
}
```

Now that they're method parameters, the scope of the three variables has been reduced to a single method. Each variable is accessible only within the `drawCircle` method. The method can be used like this:

```
Shapes shapes = new Shapes();
shapes.drawCircle(new Point(50, 50), 20, "white");
shapes.drawCircle(new Point(50, 50), 10, "black");
shapes.drawCircle(new Point(100, 50), 20, "white");
shapes.drawCircle(new Point(100, 50), 10, "black");
```

It's now easier to use because you don't have to worry about managing state when calling the method. Everything `drawCircle` needs in order to do its job is created at the beginning of the process and destroyed at the end of it. Some advantages of reducing the scope:

- You need to do less work when calling `drawCircle`, such as setting up state.

- You don't have to worry about unanticipated side effects when several methods share access to the same variable.

- You don't need to know as much about how the `Shapes` class works on the inside. You can just call its methods.

Your colleagues will prefer that you create a new variable with the narrowest scope you can. You can always expand the scope later if it becomes necessary. It's generally takes less work to expand scope than to narrow it.

Going Global

A global variable has the greatest scope of all. Such a variable is accessible by *all* parts of a program. Global variables have achieved a level of infamy similar to that of the `goto` statement (see Chapter 2), and some languages (Java included) don't support them.

The main argument favoring global variables as a cause of pandemonium really just extends the argument seen in the previous subsection: the management of a variable's state gets harder as it becomes accessible to more of your program. Global variables take this problem to the max. Eventually, you'll be overwhelmed with unmanageable behavior and flurries of unanticipated side effects.

While Java doesn't support global variables, you can pull a trick in Java that simulates all the joys of a global variable. This piece of code creates a variable called scores that's accessible anywhere in your program:

```java
class HighScores {
    public static int[] scores = new int[3];
}
```

It records the top three high scores achieved by players of a video game in the order they were achieved. The game can also output a leaderboard:

```java
class Game {
    public void showLeaderboard() {
        // Display scores in numerical order
        LeaderBoard table = new LeaderBoard();
        table.showScores();
    }
    public void showScoreHistory() {
        // Display scores in historical order
        HistoryBoard table = new HistoryBoard();
        table.showScores();
    }
}
```

Let's say three players play and score 150, 120, and 240 (in that order). The next player chooses to look at the history board (which calls the showScoreHistory method) and sees this:

1. 150

2. 120

3. 240

Then, the player chooses to look at the leaderboard (which calls the showLeaderboard method) and, as expected, sees this:

1. 240

2. 150

3. 120

But then the player chooses to look at the history board again, and something strange happens. They see this:

1. 240

2. 150

3. 120

What's gone wrong? Let's look inside the HistoryBoard class:

```
class HistoryBoard {
    public void showScores() {
        for (int i = 0; i < 3; i++) {
            System.out.println(HighScores.scores[i]);
        }
    }
}
```

Nothing surprising there. What about the LeaderBoard class?

```
class LeaderBoard {
    public void showScores() {
        Arrays.sort(HighScores.scores);
        for (int i = 0; i < 3; i++) {
            System.out.println(HighScores.scores[i]);
        }
    }
}
```

Ah-ha! The LeaderBoard sorts the scores array before displaying it. This has the undesirable side effect of destroying the old ordering, which means the HistoryBoard no longer works as expected thereafter.

Thoroughly Abuse the Type System

Programming languages offer type systems as a means of program verification. Assigning a type to a variable is one way to verify that your program uses that variable in a valid way. The type system is your friend.

But then, who needs friends?

Turn Numbers into Secret Codes

Numbers can be abused in a few interesting ways. Sensible people expect numbers to represent some kind of quantity, but, let's be honest, sensible people lack vision. In computing, we can abuse numbers and put them to more "imaginative" uses.

For example, you could make numbers mean something other than their value, turning them from things that measure quantity into your own secret codes. Take a look at this example:

```
int status_code = connect_to_device();

switch (status_code) {
    case 0:
        display_info(info_messages[1]);
        break;
    case 1:
        reattempt();
        break;
    case 2:
        display_warning(warning_messages[3]);
        break;
}
```

The function connect_to_device attempts to connect to a hardware device and afterward returns a status code. The rest of this program then decides what to do depending on the value of the code. Since it goes without saying we're not commenting our code, this leaves the reviewers scratching their heads as to what exactly is supposed to happen in each case.

As a bonus, this program also stores lists of messages in arrays, meaning they're accessible by an index number. This obscures which message is actually being referred to.

Thumbs Down!

Although these days exceptions are generally recommended over error codes for reporting problems (see Chapter 7), using status codes is still acceptable in certain contexts. Even then, it's considered helpful to make the meaning more plain to the reader.

For example, a language like Java provides enumerations. They're still numbers "behind the scenes," but they allow you to use labels in place of codes. The status codes could be replaced like so:

```
public enum DeviceStatus {
    SUCCESS = 0,
    WARNING_CONNECTION_SLOW,
    ERROR_NO_PINGBACK
}

DeviceStatus status = connect_to_device();

switch (status) {
case SUCCESS:
    display_info(info_messages[1]);
    break;
case ERROR_NO_PINGBACK:
    reattempt();
    break;
case WARNING_CONNECTION_SLOW:
    display_warning(warning_messages[3]);
    break;
}
```

Something similar can be done with the index numbers of the message collections. Instead of reading info_messages[1], it's more helpful to see something like info_messages.CONNECTION_SUCCEEDED.

Strings Are Magic—They Can Pretend to Be Any Type

Compared to most other types, strings place few limits on what they can store. Integer types limit you to numbers only. Booleans limit you to only two values. But strings allow you to store a practically unlimited array of characters. Why go to the bother of learning all the restrictions of various other types when you can just put your information into strings and do whatever you want with them?

For example, in a computer game, you might need to assign compass directions to characters in the game.

```
if (key_pressed == "Up") {
    // Our character, Zilda, now faces north
    zilda.direction = "North";
}
```

This is a nicely subtle approach because it is both simple to use and simple to get wrong. For instance, when our character uses the magical Rod of Sharathgar, he must be facing north. Hence this test:

```
public boolean canUseRod() {
    if (zilda.direction == "north") {
        return true;
    }
    return false;
}
```

At first glance, this code might seem fine, but to Java "North" and "north" are different values. Thus, this if statement will fail, even if Zilda is facing the right way, and hence he'll never be able to use his rod.

Thumbs Down!

Strings are unrestrictive because they impose little meaning onto a value. A string is just a collection of characters. The laid-back willingness of strings to store any information you want, no questions asked, means that you don't benefit from the careful validation a type system offers.

For example, if you choose a string to represent directions, possible values include not only "north," "south," "east," and "west," but also "NoRth," "soiuth," "eest," or "cuckoo."

If a string variable is supposed to hold numeric data, it won't complain if you accidentally assign to it "10O" instead of "100," and you certainly won't be able to do arithmetic with it.

Do yourself a favor. Use appropriate types that match the meaning of your data.

Mix Things Up

One advantage of collections is you can loop over their contents and apply the same operations to each item. This, you may ask, is so simple that there's no scope for mucking it up, is there?

Oh, ye of little faith.

You can do something that on the surface sounds so simple but in actuality can lead to verbose and brittle code if you do it the right (i.e., the wrong) way: include mixed types in your collection.

Normally, your colleagues expect collections to contain items belonging to only one type, so including objects of multiple types will be an unpleasant surprise for them. You need a language that supports this, and many do these days. For example, an ArrayList in Java can contain any type of object when you declare it as an ArrayList<Object>, since all types inherit from Object.

The following code, which collects patient information into a list, demonstrates:

```
ArrayList<Object> patientInfos = getPatient();

String name = (String) patientInfos.get(0);
Date dob = (Date) patientInfos.get(1);
Integer weight = (Integer) patientInfos.get(2);

System.out.println("Name: " + patientInfos.get(0));
System.out.println("Date of birth: " +
        patientInfos.get(1));
System.out.println("Weight: " + patientInfos.get(2) +
        "kg");
```

This code expects that patient information lists only ever contain string objects in position 0, date objects in position 1, and integer objects in position 2. If an object is not of the expected type, the cast from Object fails, and a runtime error occurs. As a result, an ArrayList—something that ought to be a flexible construct—is abused and turned into a more brittle, record-style structure.

In this case, it's fairly easy to make a mistake and put an object of the wrong type in the wrong position. As an added bonus, it's a mistake that compilers won't ordinarily pick up on. Objects occupying an incorrect space in the list will be revealed at runtime—with a bit of luck, after the program has shipped.

Thumbs Down!

An important skill to develop in programming is recognizing when the built-in types become insufficient for your needs and you must create your own.

The preceding example is one of many different symptoms that can indicate a program design is crying out for a new type. In this case, code that deals with several values of different types naturally clumps together. Collectively, those values describe a single entity: a patient. The example would therefore be improved by bringing those three properties together into a dedicated structure. For example, in an object-oriented program, you might create a `PatientRecord` type with methods like `getName()` and `getWeight()`.

Null—The Harbinger of Doom

Null is marvellous. It's something so dangerous and error-prone that even its own inventor has practically disowned it.

> *I call it my billion-dollar mistake. . . . My goal was to ensure that all use of references should be absolutely safe, with checking performed automatically by the compiler. But I couldn't resist the temptation to put in a null reference, simply because it was so easy to implement. This has led to innumerable errors, vulnerabilities, and system crashes, which have probably caused a billion dollars of pain and damage in the last forty years.*
>
> —Tony Hoare, 2009

While Tony Hoare may have lost his nerve as he grew older, you, on the other hand, embrace chaos. Null makes a potent weapon, so you should stick it in your arsenal.

Null Checks

Needless to say, don't perform null checks.

```
CustomerAccount c = getNextCustomer();
System.out.println(c.getSurname());
```

This reasonable-looking code gets a `CustomerAccount` object and prints out the customer's surname. However, the author was lazy (always a good approach to bad

47

programming) and didn't bother to check how the `CustomerAccount` class works. If they had, they'd have discovered that the `getSurname` method returns null if the surname was not assigned a value.

Therefore, this code is a `NullPointerException` just waiting to happen.

Seeding Disaster

When you write your own subroutines, make sure you return nulls whenever you can, especially in surprising ways.

- When you create a variable that will eventually be returned by a subroutine, initialize it to null.

- When a subroutine needs to return an "empty" value, return null.

- Don't, whatever you do, give any clues to users of the subroutine that indicate it might return null. That only increases the risk that the user will act on that knowledge to make their use of the subroutine more robust (and *robust* is a dirty word in this book!).

Thumbs Down!

The fight against null goes on. Not only are eagle-eyed reviewers on guard against its use in program code, but also programming languages are adapting to reduce its potential to cause damage.

Reviewers will watch out for certain problems in your code. If they're careful enough, they'll catch your missing null checks. They might insist on rewriting the preceding example like so:

```
CustomerAccount c = getNextCustomer();
if (c.getSurname() != null) {
    System.out.println(c.getSurname());
}
```

Of course, if you wrote the `CustomerAccount` class, they might go one better and make you change its behavior so that its properties are initialized to non-null empty values. For example, when an account has no surname, `getSurname` should return an empty string. When an account has no credit cards, `getCreditCards` should return an empty collection rather than null.

If a subroutine *must* return null, you'll be told to make that potential very clear. This can depend on the language used. For example, Java allows you to write JavaDoc comments to describe what a method might return. Such a comment should include potential null return:

```
/**
 * Looks up an account by the customer's surname.
 * @return The account object or null if the account
 *     could not be located.
 */
public CustomerAccount getAccountBySurname(
        String surname) {
    // ...
}
```

Additionally, Java supports annotations like @NotNull that indicate things like whether a variable can be null or whether a method is allowed to return null (Oracle, 2014). Tools like compilers and IDEs can ensure that your code matches the behavior promised by those annotations and report problematic code at compile-time accordingly.

Another weapon in the fight against null is the Optional type.[1] It neatly encapsulates the idea of a variable's having the potential to contain no value (i.e., be equal to null) and forces the programmer to consider what to do if that's the case. It makes the handling of potential missing values safer and easier than trying to remember to perform null checks.

In the following example, getGradeForStudent returns the grade assigned to a student taking an exam. However, it's possible that the student hasn't yet taken the exam, in which case the grade would be missing. Therefore, getGradeForStudent returns an Optional<Grade> object instead of a Grade object.

```
// maybeGrade may or may not contain a Grade
Optional<Grade> maybeGrade = getGradeForStudent(
        studentNumber);

// Call the Grade's toString method, or
// return "Unassigned" if the grade isn't present.
```

---

[1]Similar constructs in other languages are called the Maybe type.

```
String grade = maybeGrade
        .map(Grade::toString)
        .orElse("Unassigned");
System.out.println(grade);
```

Since attempting to print a variable with a null value results in an error, the Optional type can first try to get the string representation of the grade (by calling grade's toString method). If it finds the value is missing, it instead returns the value contained in the orElse method.

CHAPTER 4

Conditionals

Objectives

In this chapter, you'll learn:

- How to make poorly structured and incomplete conditionals

- How to write gnarled and error-prone expressions

- What nesting is and how you can abuse it to write complicated code

Prerequisites

Before reading this chapter, make sure you're familiar with:

- For-each loops

- Basic String methods in Java, particularly `equals`, `substring`, `length`, and `charAt`

- The basic idea behind reading files in Java

- Logical operators (`&&`, `||` and `!`)

Introduction

Conditionals (like `if` statements and `select` statements) allow the computer to choose automatically between different possibilities. They are fundamental to programming and feature in just about every language you can think of. Hence, learning how to mess up conditionals gives you anti-social skills transferrable to any project.

This chapter will demonstrate how misusing conditionals can lead a program to take the wrong action or even fail to take any action at all when it should. You'll also see how to cover your tracks and conceal such bugs among sloppy and confusing code.

© Karl Beecher 2018
K. Beecher, *Bad Programming Practices 101*, https://doi.org/10.1007/978-1-4842-3411-2_4

Forget the Alternatives

No one is so brave that he is not disturbed by something unexpected.

—Julius Caesar

A little psychology can go a long way in your pursuit of bad programming practices. Taking advantage of the biases and blind spots in human thinking helps you write problematic code without others noticing.

Or Else What?

We're all occasionally guilty of narrow thinking, considering only what we expect to be the case and failing to consider other eventualities. It's our own fault for being human. As a result of this, programmers sometimes mistakenly assume that a program will always execute as expected, or they take alternative outcomes for granted.

Unlike humans, computers don't make assumptions about alternative outcomes. They don't have the common sense to infer, for example, that if a moving elevator isn't going up then it's going down. This is why God gave us the `else` clause.

Of course, this means more work for you, having to plan out all the various conditions governing your program's execution and then explain in code how to deal with them. If you don't fancy all that work, then just don't do it. As one anti-rule of programming instructs you: *Assume nothing can go wrong.* Needless to say, avoiding the inclusion of necessary `else` clauses is a good way to build a bug-ridden program.

Here are a couple of examples to illustrate it.

You're asked to write a method that evaluates the scores from an exam attempt. It's a simple rule: if a subject scores more than 60 percent, they pass.

```
void calculateGrade(int score)
{
    if (score > 60) {
        grade = "Pass";
    }
}
```

It may be obvious to us that not passing a test with a binary outcome means to fail it, but it's not obvious to a computer. Using the preceding code to calculate a grade means that everyone who scores above 60 percent is awarded a pass and everyone else gets nothing. *Literally* nothing, not even a "Fail" grade!

Here's another example. A file called listOfSpies.txt contains the names of secret agents currently active in the field. Your code needs to output the names from that file.

```
File f = new File("listOfSpies.txt");
System.out.println("Reading listOfSpies.");
outputFileMetadata(f);
BufferedReader br = new BufferedReader(
        new FileReader(f));
String line = br.readLine();

while (line != null) {
    system.out.println(line);
    line = br.readLine();
}
```

This code will work under normal circumstances, but several assumptions are built into it, such as that the file called listOfSpies.txt actually exists. It's perfectly conceivable the file has actually gone missing (if you've seen the *Mission: Impossible* films, you'll know this kind of thing happens all the time). This code fails to account for this eventuality.

Thumbs Down!

You can usually fix such problems quite easily. For example, to ensure that failing students are actually assigned a grade, the code should be:

```
void calculateGrade(int score)
{
    if (score > 60) {
        grade = "Pass";
    }
    else {
        grade = "Fail";
    }
}
```

To account for the list of spies going missing, the code could be improved like this:

```java
File f = new File("listOfSpies.txt");
if (! f.exists()) {
    System.out.println("List of spies is missing!");
    setAlertLevel("Oh f**k!");
}
else {
    outputFileMetadata(f);
    System.out.println("Reading listOfSpies.");
    BufferedReader br = new BufferedReader(
            new FileReader(f));
    String line = br.readLine();
    while (line != null) {
        System.out.println(line);
        line = br.readLine();
    }
}
```

You might think this is all quite obvious advice and that professional programmers would never make such mistakes . . . but you'd be mistaken. This kind of oversight happens surprisingly often. In fact, one classic study found that 50–80 percent of if statements in professionally written software under analysis should have had a corresponding else clause (Elshoff, 1976).

Some programming manuals even recommend you consider adding else clauses to if statements as a matter of habit, even if the else clause ends up empty, just to show that you've considered the alternative (McConnell, 2004).[1]

The Normal and the Exceptional

Here's some more psychology knowledge to abuse. Humans have certain intuitive preferences when considering normal cases and exceptional cases: they tend to prefer considering the expected outcome first *before* considering any exceptions (Pane and Myers, 2001).

---

[1]Personally, I think sticking rigidly to such a rule is overkill, but it's *always* worth at least considering the else clause.

Reversing this wisdom—putting exceptional cases before normal cases—means your code works counter to the reader's expectation. The previous example that kept track of spies is guilty of this, but it only scratched the surface of the mess-making potential. Consider this extended version:

```
File f = new File("listOfSpies.txt");
if (! f.exists()) {
    System.out.println("List of spies is missing!");
    setAlertLevel("Oh f**k!");
}
else
{
    System.out.println("Reading listOfSpies.");
    if (! f.canRead()) {
        // Don't have permission to read it!
        System.out.println("Can't read file! Are you a foreign spy?");
    }
    else {
        outputFileMetadata(f);
        if (f.length() == 0) {
            // The file is empty!
            System.out.println("List is empty!");
        }
        else {
            BufferedReader br = new BufferedReader(
                    new FileReader(f));
            String line = br.readLine();
            while (line != null) {
                outputAgent(line);
                line = br.readLine();
            }
        }
    }
}
```

The example is now a chain of decisions, each one dealing with a new exceptional case.

Actually, it contains two counts of bad practice. Yes, it leads with the exceptional cases, but also notice how the code from the normal case has now been broken up and intermingled with the various exceptional cases? This prevents the reader from being able to consider one case at a time. It forces them to shift constantly between normal cases and exceptional cases as they try (and hopefully fail) to comprehend the code.

Thumbs Down!

Code becomes more readable when it takes human habits into account. Various ways exist to make code like this more readable.

For example, you could rewrite the chain of cases so that it respects human intuition by leading with the normal case:

```java
File f = new File("listOfSpies.txt");
if (f.exists()) {
    outputFileMetadata(f);
    if (f.canRead()) {
        System.out.println("Reading listOfSpies.");
        if (f.length() > 0) {
            BufferedReader br = new BufferedReader(
                    new FileReader(f));
            String line = br.readLine();
            while (line != null) {
                System.out.println(line);
                line = br.readLine();
            }
        }
        // Before now, everything was normal
        // Afterward, everything is exceptional
        else {
            System.out.println("List of spies is empty!");
        }
    }
    else {
        System.out.println("Can't read file!");
    }
}
```

```
else {
    System.out.println("List of spies is missing!");
}
```

Not bad, but this approach is vulnerable to overly deep nesting as the number of conditions grows.

Alternatively, you could use guard clauses. Doing this separates out all the exceptional cases into a series of if statements—each of which checks whether executing the normal case is impossible—and puts them at the beginning of the subroutine.

```
File f = new File("listOfSpies.txt");

// Three guard clauses follow
if (! f.exists()) {
    System.out.println("List of spies is missing!");
    return;
}

if (! f.canRead()) {
    System.out.println("Can't read file!");
    return;
}

if (f.length() == 0) {
    System.out.println("List of spies is empty!");
    return;
}

// Business as usual
System.out.println("Reading listOfSpies.");
outputFileMetadata(f);
BufferedReader br = new BufferedReader(
        new FileReader(f));
String line = br.readLine();
while (line != null) {
    outputAgent(line);
    line = br.readLine();
}
```

Essentially, each guard clause is a precondition for deciding whether to proceed with the subroutine or to bail out of business as usual because of a problem.

Build a Ladder

Sometimes a routine involves choosing between lots of mutually exclusive alternatives. The decision process might be described as follows: "If A is the case, then do this; otherwise, if B is the case, do that; otherwise, if it's C, do the other . . . etc., etc."

By doing minimal planning, you can simply put the code into a structure that matches the description without thinking it through any further. In this case, an `if` ladder. For example:

```
if (item.getType().equals("scannable")) {
    price = item.scanBarcode();
}
else if (item.getType().equals("produce")) {
    price = item.weigh();
}
else if (item.getType.equals("reduced")) {
    price = item.keyInPrice();
}
// etc...
```

Reactively choosing an `if` ladder without serious thought means you're protected against choosing better alternatives.

Thumbs Down!

Short `if` ladders rarely pose serious problems, but when they start growing really long, that usually means you need to find a better design. It comes down partly to readability (long ladders are not particularly nice to read), but also partly to complexity and design.

Figure 4-1 models the `if` ladder from the previous example using a flow-control diagram (introduced in Chapter 2) so you can more clearly visualize its complexity.

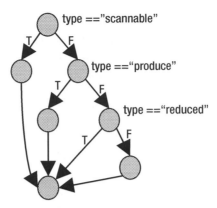

type =="scannable"

T   F

type =="produce"

T   F

type =="reduced"

T   F

Figure 4-1. *Flow-control diagram of an example if ladder*

An alternative structure in these situations could be the switch statement. This signals more clearly to the reader the intent of choosing between multiple alternatives and cuts down on code clutter.

```
switch (item.getType()) {
    case "scannable":
        price = item.scanBarcode();
        break;
    case "produce":
        price = item.weigh();
        break;
    case "reduced":
        price = item.keyInPrice();
        break;
    // etc.
}
```

The flow-control diagram of the switch statement shows how it is also simpler in form than an if ladder (Figure 4-2).

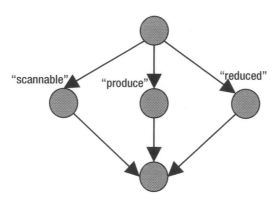

Figure 4-2. *Flow-control diagram of a switch statement*

However, you should be cautious with switch statements. They vary in exact behavior between programming languages. In fact, switch statements in some languages (like Java and C/C++) can get quite messy if used poorly. For example, by omitting the break statement at the end of each case, a switch statement becomes a glorified goto statement.

When using an object-oriented language, you could also consider taking advantage of polymorphism as a more effective alternative to both if ladders and switch statements.[2]

Abuse Expressions

In programming, an expression is a combination of values, variables, operators, or function calls. It can be evaluated to return a computed value. For example, 1+3 is an expression. So is x*2 or pi*getRadius()*getRadius().

Expressions are essential to making decisions, since a program has to evaluate them when deciding what to do next.

Tortuous Expressions

Expressions can become arbitrarily long and complex. A couple of anti-rules (*In general, the bigger the better* and *Complex is better than simple*) tell us what to do with that insight: make them long and complex. Only your imagination limits how tortuous you can make an expression, so get dreaming.

---

[2]Polymorphism will be covered in Chapter 9.

You could, for example, make expressions cluttered (code clutter having been discussed in Chapter 2). Adding extraneous, complicated, or unnecessary code can overwhelm the reader and frustrate their attempts to understand it.

Take this example, which validates a SWIFT code[3] by encoding the rules into an expression:

```
// e.g., "DEUTDEF1XXX"
String code = getSwiftCode();

// L or T depending on live or test
String mode = getMode();

if (((code.length() == 8 || code.length() == 11)) && (code.substring(4,6).
equals("DE")) && ((mode + code.charAt(7)).equals("L1") || (mode + code.
charAt(7)).equals("L2")))) {
    // Code checks out
}
```

Do you find that hard to understand? Good—it's supposed to be. And if anyone complains, you can simply reply, "Validating SWIFT codes is complicated, so it's a complicated expression. What can *I* do about it?"

Thumbs Down!

In fact, you can do things to make expressions more readable, even if they describe complicated ideas. Indeed, you'll be *expected* to when they get really messy. Some reasons why the last expression is hard to read:

- Too much is packed onto a single line.

- An excessive number of parentheses add to the confusion.

- Subexpressions, which could be assigned to an intermediate value, are instead repeatedly evaluated (e.g., `mode + code.charAt(7)`).

Here's how we could remove those problems and make the expression easier to read.

First, those repeated subexpressions could be put into an intermediate value. In this case, `mode + code.charAt(7)` becomes the variable `tag`.

[3]A SWIFT code uniquely identifies organizations (e.g., financial institutions) in international transactions.

```
String code = getSwiftCode();
String tag = getMode() + mode.charAt(7);

if ((((code.length() == 8 || code.length() == 11)) && (code.substring(4,6).
equals("DE")) && ((tag).equals("L1") || (tag).equals("L2"))) {
    // ...
}
```

Then, we could separate out the individual rules and put each on its own line (as recommended by CA-CST, 2015):

```
String code = getSwiftCode();
String tag = getMode() + mode.charAt(7);

if ((((code.length() == 8 || code.length() == 11)) &&
    (code.substring(4,6).equals("DE")) &&
    ((tag).equals("L1") || (tag).equals("L2"))) {
    // ...
}
```

Next, individual rules could be moved into their own subroutines and be replaced with method calls (as recommended by Martin, 2009):

```
String code = getSwitfCode();
String tag = getMode() + mode.charAt(7);

if (((validLength(code))) &&
    (validCountry(code) &&
    (validMode(code, tag)) {
    // ...
}

// ...

private boolean validLength(String code) {
    return code.length() == 8 || code.length() == 11
}

private boolean validCountry(String code) {
    return code.substring(4,6).equals("DE");
}
```

```
private boolean validMode(String code, String
        tag) {
    return tag.equals("L1") || tag.equals("L2");
}
```

This not only shortens the expression, but the function names also add relevant semantic information. Also, the extraneous parentheses now look really obvious.

```
if (validLength(code) &&
    validCountry(code) &&
    validMode(code, tag))
```

These simple steps have gone a long way to improving the readability of the expression.

Not Being Not Non-negative . . . Not

Sir Humphrey Appleby: We could not know that you would deny it in the House.

James Hacker: Well, obviously I would if I didn't know and I were asked.

Appleby: We did not know that you would be asked when you didn't know.

Hacker: But I was bound to be asked when I didn't know if I didn't know.

Appleby: What?

—*Yes, Minister*, Series 1, Episode 3

Do you not think that not being non-negative is an ineffective way of not writing confusing code? If you understand this question enough to have a response, then please send an explanation to me, because I don't understand it and I wrote the darned thing.

The fact is, humans tend to struggle with excessive negation. Here's the good news: the fun you can have sowing confusion with double, triple, and quadruple negatives in natural language applies to programming languages too. Take this example of a main control loop for a tic-tac-toe game.[4] As long as the condition holds true, the game keeps going:

```
while (!(squaresUnavailable == 9 || !noLinesAchieved)) {
    // next turn...
}
```

[4]A.K.A. Noughts and Crosses

63

The condition reads something like, "Loop while it is not the case that the number of unavailable squares equals 9 nor is it not true that no lines have been achieved."

It expresses the rules of the game correctly, but it sounds like something from the mouth of Sir Humphrey Appleby. The variables are expressed negatively, one of them is also directly negated, and the whole expression itself is then further negated. If you find this all a bit tricky to process mentally, that's just because you're human. If you want to confuse and frustrate you colleagues, then write expressions with excessive negativity (assuming they're human too).

Thumbs Down!

Whether or not you're a misanthrope in real life, you should dial down the negativity in your expressions because humans deal better with positively phrased ones.

If you find that your excessively negative expressions cause people to perform extreme mental contortions, you could consider rephrasing your expressions more positively. One tool to help you is a rule in logic called De Morgan's Law. It states that, in a condition that contains two clauses (A and B), you can:

1. Flip the negation of both clauses, then,

2. switch the *or* relation to an *and* (or switch the *and* relation to an *or*) and then negate the whole condition.

In purely logical terms:

> *not A or not B*

is equivalent to saying

> *not (A and B).*

It's also true that

> *not A and not B*

is the same as saying

> *not (A or B).*

Applying De Morgan's Law to the preceding example means we could express the same rule differently and a bit more intuitively:

```
while (squaresUnavailable != 9 && noLinesAchieved)
```

We could also consider making the variables express information more positively too:

```
while (squaresAvailable > 0 && !linesAchieved)
```

Include Gaps and Overlaps

Dealing with ranges provides fertile ground for errors. The ease with which we unintentionally overlap ranges or overlook gaps in them can cause havoc. Let's see how we can harness that havoc.

As a demonstration, this section will revisit the earlier example of grading examinations, but this time the examination has more nuanced scoring, awarding the standard A to F grades as appropriate.

```
if (score < 40) { grade = "F"; }
else if (score > 40) { grade = "E"; }
else if (score > 50) { grade = "D"; }
else if (score > 60) { grade = "C"; }
else if (score > 70) { grade = "B"; }
else if (score > 80) { grade = "A"; }
```

Of course, we only want to make the code *appear* to be correct at a glance. This little snippet actually contains some bugs.

First of all, it contains a gap in its matching. The cut-off points for each grade should be obvious (more than 80 percent awards an A, above 70 percent bags a B and so on, right down to a fail for less than 40 percent). Notice that all possible scores are accounted for in this scheme . . . except for 40 percent. Anyone scoring exactly 40 percent will end up with no grade at all.

The second bug takes advantage of the fact that programmers can sometimes neglect to think of code as being executed step by step and instead see a chain of if statements as something like a set of rules. This is an especially common oversight among beginners (Pane and Myers, 2001).

Let's run through a couple of test executions. Say someone scores 43.

- The first clause (if (score < 40)) fails.

- The second clause (else if (score > 40)) succeeds. The correct grade, "E", is granted. The rest of the if statement is ignored.

Now, say someone scores 58.

- The first clause (if (score < 40)) fails.

- The second clause (if (score > 40)) succeeds. The student is awarded a grade "E," and the rest of the if statement is ignored. However, it matched prematurely. An "E" will be awarded, but we know a score of 58 percent should yield a "D."

Thumbs Down!

The first error in the example arose because not all values in the possible range match against an appropriate action. We'll see a possible fix in a moment.

The second bug arose because the conditions for matching the score within a range were not restrictive enough. Testing if the score is above 80 covers all scores between 80 and 100. Testing if the score is above 40 covers all scores between 40 and 100. There are two ways you could arrange the conditions more appropriately:

1. When you list the conditions to match against, start from the *most* restrictive and proceed from there down to the least restrictive. Or,

2. Express each condition with both a lower and an upper range (e.g., if (score > 40 && score <= 50)).

Choosing the first approach, a new version of the snippet that fixes both bugs would look like this.

```
if (score > 80) { grade = "A"; }
else if (score > 70) { grade = "B"; }
else if (score > 60) { grade = "C"; }
else if (score > 50) { grade = "D"; }
else if (score > 40) { grade = "E"; }
else if (score <= 40) { grade = "F"; }
// since any score not above 40 is a fail,
// the last line could also be:
// else { grade = "F"; }
```

This also fixes the first bug by changing the condition for grade "F" to score <= 40. Now, no more gaps or overlaps exist.

CHAPTER 5

Loops

Objectives

In this chapter, you'll learn:

- How to match different types of loops to the wrong situations
- How to make your program prone to freezing by incorporating infinite loops
- How to compromise the structuredness of loops
- Various ways to make loops excessively long and complex

Prerequisites

Before reading this chapter, make sure you're familiar with:

- Loops in Java:
    - For loop
    - Foreach loop
    - While (or do while) loop
- The basic idea of collections (e.g., List, Set, Queue)
- Iterators
- Reading keyboard input using the Scanner class

© Karl Beecher 2018

K. Beecher, *Bad Programming Practices 101*, https://doi.org/10.1007/978-1-4842-3411-2_5

Introduction

Like conditionals, loops are a fundamental control structure in programming. Also like conditionals, they come in a variety of "flavors" to choose from. However, loops are a more complex beast than conditionals are and, as such, have greater potential for bringing turmoil and destruction to your programs.

This chapter will discuss some basic ways of tapping into this potential.

Choose the Wrong Type

Most programming languages offer several variants of loops. They all do basically the same thing—execute the same bunch of instructions repeatedly—so there's nothing to choose between them, right?

Wrong. Once you know which situation each variant is suited for, you can then use each one inappropriately, which will increase both the chances of introducing bugs and the annoyance levels of your colleagues. Which of these two outcomes gives you greater pleasure remains your business.

Collections

Some programming languages come with built-in support for collections,[1] a term that covers a range of different data structures that all work in different ways. Java has quite a few of them, prominent examples including:

```
List<Grocery> shoppingList;
Set<Animal> pets;
Queue<Person> reallyLongLineAtTheSupermarket;
```

A lot of the time, you need to loop through a collection. So, out of all the options, which is the best loop variant to use in each situation? If you believe each variant is essentially the same, you could just as well throw a dart at a board to choose which one to use.

Hey, what a great idea!

---

[1]A collection is a data structure that brings together a list of related items under one name.

Let's say your task is to print out the price of each grocery item in a shopping list. Then, pick up the dart. Here goes . . .

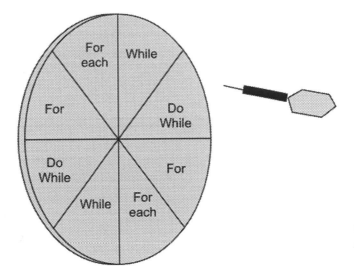

Figure 5-1. *Loop-choosing dartboard*

Oh look, it chose a for loop (Figure 5-1). Here's a for loop version of traversing a List:

```
for (int i = 0; i < shoppingList.size(); i++) {
    Grocery g = shoppingList.get(i);
    System.out.println(g.getPrice());
}
```

That works. So, for loops are good for collections, right?

Thumbs Down!

This approach uses a loop counter, i, to keep track of the current position in the collection. A couple of general problems exist with this approach.

First, not all collections can be accessed in this manner. A Set, for example, has no ordering, unlike a List. That means items in a Set have no position and so can't be accessed directly; hence, a Set has no get method.

```
for (int i = 0; i < pets.size(); i++) {
    Pet p = // uh-oh, what now?
}
```

Second, using a `for` loop necessitates maintaining a loop counter (this chore is usually referred to as housekeeping work). In the case of collections, it's actually unnecessary because `foreach` loops will take care of housekeeping work for you. They will also give you access to individual elements in a collection extremely easily.

```
for (Pet p : pets) {
    p.feed();
}
```

Being relieved of housekeeping work removes the risk of your doing it incorrectly and introducing a bug. In this case, the loop counter, `i`, must be initialized, tested, and updated all in the correct manner. Doing any of them incorrectly risks the program's causing an error.[2]

Ranges

Take your dart once more and throw it at the board before finding out what our next task is. (Yes, that might be the wrong way around, but we are trying to make a mess here!)

This time, you hit the `while` loop.

OK, here's the task: Find all the FizzBuzzes[3] between 1 and 100. Normally, for a task that requires you to iterate a fixed number of times—and possibly in steps not equal to 1—a `for` loop is recommended. First, look at the sensible version your colleagues would probably prefer you wrote:

```
for (int i = 5; i <= 100; i += 5) {
    if (i % 3 == 0) {
        System.out.println(i);
    }
}
```

---

[2]It's a not uncommon mistake to use the wrong comparison in the test part of a `for` loop. For example, '`i <= pets.size()`' would cause the program to crash with an `IndexOutOfBoundsException`.

[3]A FizzBuzz is a number that is cleanly divisible by both 3 and 5. It's a concept from the game for children (and drunken adults) of the same name.

And here is the `while` loop version:

```
int i = 5;
while (i <= 100) {
    if (i % 3 == 0) {
        System.out.println(i);
        i += 5;
    }
}
```

I'm willing to bet that the deliberate mistake in the `while`-loop version passed a few readers by. If you didn't spot it, go back and look again. I'll wait.

Did you see the problem? The part that increments the loop counter (`i += 5`) is in the wrong place. It should be *outside* the `if` block. In its current position, `i` won't ever be incremented, and the program will enter an infinite loop.

Thumbs Down!

It's not that the `while` loop is a *really* poor choice in this case, it's just that it exposes you more readily to making a simple mistake—albeit one that kills the program dead.

In both the `for`-loop and `while`-loop versions, some housekeeping code was necessary. However, whereas the `for` loop allows you to consolidate it all in one place (which also makes the intention of the loop clearer), the `while` loop often requires you to spread those steps around. This increases the chance that you put them in the wrong place or even forget them entirely. In larger loops, it can also mean that the reader has to go hunting through reams of instructions to find that housekeeping code.

Arbitrary Iterations

The next task is to print out the contents of a file line by line. Only one type of loop remains on our dartboard for this: the `foreach` loop.

Iterating over the lines of a file is an example of looping an arbitrary number of times because you don't know ahead of time how many loops need to be performed. At first glance, a `foreach` loop might unfortunately seem like a good idea, since it traverses a collection blindly from beginning to end.

Granted, you have to put that file into a collection (since `foreach` loops work only with collections), but you can still make it work.

```
List<String> lines = Files.readAllLines(
        Paths.get(filename), StandardCharsets.UTF_8);

for (String line : lines) {
    // Do stuff with that line of the file
}
```

If you're worried we've accidentally done something right, don't panic: this approach sneaks in a potential problem. The program stuffs the collection `lines` with the entire contents of the file all at once. Hence, the whole file is read into memory. If the file happens to be a rather *large* file, your program will suddenly become a memory hog. Or, even better, it will crash because the file size exceeds the amount of memory available.

Another type of program that loops arbitrarily is one that presents an interactive prompt to the user. An example of this is a text-based adventure game.[4] Playing them resembles something like this:

```
You are in a forest clearing. You see a mailbox here.

What now?> examine mailbox
It's closed.

What now?> open mailbox
You open the mailbox.

What now?> look in mialbox
I don't understand 'mialbox'.

What now?> obviously I meant mailbox
I don't understand 'obviously.'

What now?> open mailbox
A hairy, poisonous spider scuttles out of the mailbox and bites your hand.

You're dead. Your score was 0 out 500. Thanks for playing.
```

---

[4]A.K.A. Interactive fiction. To find out more about these, you might have to ask your more fossilized colleagues, who possibly played such games in their misspent youth.

Behind the scenes, the program works by repeatedly executing the following steps:

1. Print "What now?> ".

2. Read user input from keyboard.

3. Process user input.

4. Output response to user.

5. Go back to Step 1, unless the input was 'quit'.

This approach is known as a REPL (read-eval-print loop). A foreach loop would suit this approach *particularly* badly, since a program couldn't read the entirety of the user input into a collection in realtime because the user wouldn't even entered have it yet!

Thumbs Down!

Unlike iterating over collections and ranges, arbitrary looping doesn't go from a defined start point to a defined end point. Instead, it continues to execute steps until a loop exit condition is met. In cases of arbitrary looping, a while loop is more appropriate because it checks that condition at the start of each iteration.[5]

In the case of reading I/O, a while loop can process data incrementally, repeatedly going to the I/O source and reading in just a chunk of the data until no more remains. Consequently, the program doesn't have to load *all* data into memory at once. In the case of reading a file, a while loop can process it one line at a time.

```
BufferedReader fileReader = new BufferedReader(
        new FileReader(file));
String line = fileReader.readLine();

while (line != null) {
    // Do stuff with that line of the file.
    // ...

    // Get next line
    line = fileReader.readLine();
}
```

---

[5]Or at the end, in the case of the do-while loop.

In the case of an REPL for an adventure game, the loop would look something like this:

```
Scanner keyboard = new Scanner(System.in);
do {
    System.out.print("What now?> ");
    input = keyboard.next();
    String response = processInput(input);
    System.out.println(response);
} while (! input.equals("quit"));
```

Have Fun with Infinite Loops

This must have happened to you before: one minute, you're using an application. The next, it freezes and becomes unresponsive. No matter how many times you click the mouse or play a glissando on your keyboard, it refuses to come back.

Oh, how you wish you could write software as annoying as that.

But wait. You can! There's a good chance that your "frozen" program was actually stuck in an infinite loop, executing the same instructions over and over without making any progress. It's actually quite straightforward to trap a program in a loop—so easy, even the pros do it accidentally from time to time.

Citing the Masters

Here's a fun fact: did you know there's no general way to determine ahead of time whether a loop will actually terminate? It's one of the most famous discoveries from computer science, made by no less a man than the "godfather" of computing, Alan Turing, in 1937.

This means you have a powerful ally on your side if your colleagues suspect an infinite loop lurks in your code. Any time they raise the possibility, you can just throw the ball right back into your colleagues' court. Cite Turing's discovery and point out that *every* loop is potentially an infinite loop, and it is impossible to prove otherwise.

Then, you can ask them why they're picking on you and singling you out for no reason.

Thumbs Down!

Saying that no method exists for verifying loops *in general* doesn't mean we can't look at specific loops and convince ourselves they might have the potential to become stuck. The key is to verify the *logical completeness* of the loop (in other words, make sure all possible states of the data and their consequences are considered).

For example, will this simple for loop ever get stuck?

```
for (int i = 1; i < 10; j++) {
    System.out.println("Step number " + i);
}
```

Yes, it will. We can easily convince ourselves the loop condition (i < 10), which starts off true, never becomes false because its state doesn't change at all (notice that the increment changes a different variable, j, which has nothing to do with the loop's behavior).

What about the following loop, which prints out the leap years for the next fifty years. Will it get stuck?

```
int i = 0;
int year = 2016;
while (i < 50) {
    if (isLeapYear(year + i)) {
        System.out.println(i + " is a leap year");
    }
    i++;
}
```

We can easily convince ourselves it won't (assuming the isLeapYear subroutine doesn't itself contain an infinite loop). The loop is controlled by the value of i; so long as it is below 50, the loop continues. Once the loop has started, the value of i (initially 0) increases with every iteration of the loop, eventually equaling 50 and causing the loop to terminate.

Altering the loop only slightly can turn it into an infinite loop:

```
int i = 0;
int year = 2016;
while (i < 50) {
```

```
    if (isLeapYear(year + i)) {
        System.out.println(i + " is a leap year");
        i++;
    }
}
```

In this case, i's value may or may not change depending on the if statement. Let's consider the states of the data. Initially, i is 0 and year is 2016, isLeapYear will be true, therefore i will be incremented. But when i is 1, the argument to isLeapYear will be 2017. This call will return false and so i's value will remain 1. From then on, there are no other ways to alter the values of year or i, thus the loop will never end.

Some loops are only *potentially* infinite loops. Under some conditions they loop endlessly, under others they don't. It can be hard to detect the conditions leading to infinite loops, even for the pros. Here's a real-world example[6] from the code of the Microsoft Zune media player (Long, 2013). It contains a loop that gets stuck only under very specific conditions:

```
// This is the epoch year, in this case 1980
year = 1980;

public void convertDays(int days) {
    while (days > 365) {
        if (isLeapYear(year)) {
            if (days > 366) {
                days -= 366;
                year += 1;
            }
        }
        else {
            days -= 365;
            year += 1;
        }
    }
}
```

---

[6]With some slight adaptations to make it more Java-like.

This method takes the days variable (which always contains the current number of days since January 1, 1980) and computes the current year and day numbers. Most of time, the code works fine.

But can you find where the code is logically incomplete? Since the execution of the while loop depends on the value of days being continually decremented, is there a path through the code where this doesn't happen?

Yes: when isLeapYear returns true and days is *not* greater than 366.

Ask yourself what would happen—indeed, what *did* happen—to people trying to listen to their Zune players on December 30, 2008? Or, to put it another way, on the 365th day of the leap year 2008?

Answer: a lot of music lovers were angry because their media player had inexplicably frozen.

Taking Precautions

Now that you've seen how ignoring certain data states can cause endless looping, your fiendish brain is probably learning from that and trying to work out how to apply that knowledge in your programs without anyone else noticing.

One way to do this is to restrict the scope of a loop condition unnecessarily. Let's look again at our leap-year example. Notice that the while loop condition has been altered from while (i < 50):

```
int i = 0;
int year = 2016;
while (i != 50) {
    if (isLeapYear(year + i)) {
        System.out.println(i + " is a leap year");
    }
    i++;
}
```

It's a small change, easily missed, and it doesn't introduce an infinite loop. However, this new loop condition is less cautious than the old one, and it sows the seeds of a potential infinite loop should further changes be made to the code in the future. For now though, the code still works, and an infinite loop is sure to be avoided.

But read on to see the fruits of this seed you planted . . .

Thumbs Down!

The original condition in our leap-year example (`while (i < 50)`) was *stronger* since it took into account far more data states. Any value of i equal to or above 50 will terminate the loop. However, `while (i != 50)` considers only one value as sufficient for terminating a loop, making it a significantly weaker condition.

Picking a range of values as a loop terminator rather than a specific value is merely a precaution, but a very useful one (Kernighan and Plauger, 1978). For example, someone might subsequently optimize the loop, reasoning that leap years occur at least every four years and so there's no need to check the years in-between. Thus, the loop increment is increased from 1 to 4:

```java
int i = 0;
int year = 2016;
while (i != 50) {
    if (isLeapYear(year + i)) {
        System.out.println(i + " is a leap year");
    }
    i += 4;
}
```

However, i will now never become equal to 50. It will progress from 0 to 4 to 8, and so on, up to 48 and then jump over 50 to 52. From there on, the loop will continue endlessly. The original, stronger condition didn't suffer from this problem because it established a ceiling value, any value above which would terminate the loop.

Another precaution worth considering is a safety counter, which specifies an upper limit on the number of iterations a loop may carry out. You can set the value of the safety counter to an easily reachable yet nevertheless clearly excessive value. When the loop goes beyond the chosen safety limit, that indicates it's gone infinite, and so the loop is immediately ended.

The following example shows a journey planner, which goes through all possible routes from place A to place B until it finds one satisfying the user's preferred maximum duration.

```java
Route suggestedRoute = null;
int counter = 0;
while (suggestedRoute == null) {
```

```
    Route possibleRoute = routeFinder.getNextRoute();
    if (possibleRoute.getDuration() < maxDuration) {
        suggestedRoute = possibleRoute;
    }
    counter++;
    if (counter > SAFETY_LIMIT) {
        System.err.println(
            "Exceeded limit searching for routes.");
        break;
    }
}
```

It contains some potential problems that might prevent the loop from exiting:

- The `routeFinder.getNextRoute()` method might keep returning the same set of unacceptable routes over and over.

- If a sufficient number of intermediate locations exist between A and B, combinatorial explosion means that the number of possible routes can grow staggeringly large, big enough that the computer can be tied up for years (literally!) searching through all the possibilities.[7]

A safety counter ensures that the computer gives up before it searches for too long. In this example, the counter is checked by the final `if` statement.

Make Inappropriate Exits

As Chapter 2 pointed out, the motivation behind structured loops is to avoid a chaotic flow of control. That's why loops are supposed to have single entry and exit points.

However, the designers of certain programming languages very kindly gave us ways to circumvent these restrictions. They probably believed that programmers would use them wisely and responsibly.

Excuse me while I break into evil laughter.

---

[7]Technically, this wouldn't be an infinite loop since the program would end eventually, but the user is probably unwilling to wait a few thousand years for that.

Break Out

Why is it, when you're looking for something, it's always in the last place you look?

—Popular (and kinda dumb) phrase

"What if I need to bail out of a loop early?"

It's a fair question, isn't it? After all, you don't need to keep searching for something once you've found it.

The answer depends on who's asking.

When a sensible programmer asks the question, they're inquiring whether a sensible method exists. Of course, when *you* ask the question, you want the easy way, one that requires little thought, annoys your co-workers, and (fingers crossed) makes a program susceptible to error.

So, the answer to *your* question is simple: just bail out wherever you like. In fact, go crazy. Dump break or continue statements throughout a loop. Each one adds another exit point to a loop and makes it less structured.

Look at this example, which loops through a collection of snacks looking for the first acceptable one:

```
while (true) {
    // If it's chocolate, I want it!
    if (currentSnack.getType().equals("Chocolate")) {
        chosenSnack = currentSnack;
        break;
    }
    // Otherwise, I'll take a biscuit if it doesn't
    // contain gluten.
    else if (currentSnack.getType().equals("Biscuit")) {
        boolean containsGluten =
                allergiesInfo.hasGluten(currentSnack);
        if (!containsGluten) {
            chosenSnack = currentSnack;
            break;
        }
    }
}
```

```
if (snackIterator.hasNext()) {
    // This didn't satisfy me, move to next one
    currentSnack = snackIterator.next();
}
else {
    // Didn't find any snacks at all!
    break;
}
}
```

This loop shows how you can take a fairly simple task and make it overly complex. The simple search loop has three different exit points and an if-else that could easily grow into an if ladder[8] as the array of snacks on offer grows.

Thumbs Down!

Multiple exit points make a routine more complicated and force the reader to look carefully inside a loop to understand how it is controlled. Things get particularly complicated when you spread exit points around among various other pieces of code, rendering them more easily missed.

The jury is out over the best way to handle situations like this. Some recommend avoiding break statements in favor of setting a flag, which can then be checked as part of a for loop (e.g., Mughal et al, 2007). Others claim that using a break statement is fine as a last resort, and that all conditions leading up to an early exit should be consolidated into one, clear position in the loop (e.g., McConnell, 2004).

Here's an example following the former advice:

```
// Using a for loop means you don't need to do iterator
// housekeeping and consolidates all exits points
// into one places.
for (int i = 0;
    chosenSnack == null && i < snacks.size();
    i++) {
    currentSnack = snacks.get(i);
```

---

[8]Chapter 4 discussed if ladders.

```
    // Remember! A break statement in a switch only jumps
    // out of the switch. It doesn't exit the loop!
    switch (currentSnack.getType()) {
        case "Chocolate":
            chosenSnack = currentSnack;
            break;
        case "Biscuit":
            if (allergiesInfo.hasGluten(currentSnack)) {
                chosenSnack = currentSnack;
            }
            break;
    }
}
```

Make 'em Looooong and Complex

This book has already discussed the effects of size and complexity on your code. This section will apply that discussion specifically to loops.

Long Loops

Chapter 2 first mentioned the anti-rule *"In general, the bigger the better"* when pointing out how making routines long can have negative effects on them. The good news is, this applies to loops as well.

Like long subroutines, long loops force the reader to manage a lot of detail in their fragile little brain all at once. Trying and failing to keep track of numerous details (whose state continually changes) is how bugs often go overlooked. Writing long loops keeps those details numerous.

But loops can derive another problem from growing long. A loop often requires some housekeeping code that controls its execution, like loop-counter incrementations. As the earlier section "Have Fun with Infinite Loops" explained, if this housekeeping code mismanages the data controlling the loop, it can drive the program into an infinite loop. By splitting the housekeeping code and spreading it around a long loop, you make it harder to locate and keep track of that code, upping the chance that the reader will miss a problem.

It's a particularly nice touch if you write a loop too long to fit on screen. That means the reader can't view it all at once and can end up being further distracted by the constant need to scroll and search.

Thumbs Down!

There's no rule regarding the maximum length of a loop, but some textbooks and coding standards use the screen size as a rule of thumb. Most screens can fit roughly fifty lines of code (notwithstanding some of the exotic sizes and configurations of monitors nowadays), so it's claimed a loop shouldn't exceed that length (McConnell, 2004).

When a loop starts getting too long, you'll be expected to take steps to curtail that length. You could look at the design of the loop and see whether you are trying to pack too much into it. Perhaps you could break the long loop into a series of shorter, clearer loops.

Alternatively, you could apply the same advice from Chapter 2 regarding long subroutines: break the contents up into chunks of code and move each into a separate subroutine, replacing each chunk with a call to that new subroutine. Video games are a good example of this. They typically have a central control loop that continually updates every aspect of the game world. This loop executes as long as the game runs. For a large game, you can imagine just how much stuff needs updating.

```
while (game.isRunning()) {
    // ...
    // Lots of code for checking user input
    // ...
    // Lots of code for updating position
    // of each object in the game world
    // ...
    // Lots of code for detecting
    // collisions between objects
    // ...
    // Lots of code for possibly creating
    // new objects
}
```

Instead of hundreds of lines of detailed code, the reader would be better off seeing a series of calls, like this:

```
while (game.isRunning()) {
    getUserInput();
    updatePositions();
    detectCollisions();
    createNewObjects();
}
```

Complex Loops

Research shows that loops don't come naturally to humans (Pane and Myers, 2001). That means, if you want to make loops complex and difficult to understand (as per the anti-rule *"Prefer complex over simple,"*) you already have a head start. If you layer on the complexity in a loop, you're making a difficult spot in a program even harder to understand. So, don't miss a chance to really pack a loop full of complexity.

Things you can try include the following:

- Spreading the housekeeping code around the loop. Don't bunch it all in one place (as per the anti-rule, *"Spread stuff around and duplicate, don't consolidate things."*).

- Include lots of `break` and `continue` statements. They increase the number of possible pathways through the loop, adding to the programmer's mental load.

- Increase the level of nesting. Excessive nesting is particularly problematic inside a loop.

Thumbs Down!

This whole book contains advice for managing (as well as *mismanaging*) complexity. Much of it applies equally to loops.

As for complexity particular to loops, a good start is to do the opposite of the anti-advice above:

- Keep housekeeping code in one place.

- Ideally, a loop should have one exit point.

- Keep depth of nesting restricted. The recommended maximum is around three or four levels (Yourdon, 1986).

Your colleagues will appreciate stuff like this.

Something else you might consider is ditching a loop altogether for a different approach. Loops are a step-by-step, "one-object-at-a-time" approach. They're often imposed on us by programming languages, but studies show that they're unintuitive and tricky to handle, especially for less-experienced programmers (Pane and Myers, 2001).

One alternative is provided by the functional programming approach, which allows collections of things to be dealt with without framing everything in terms of looping. Such an approach describes *what* is done to all items collectively, rather than *how* things are done to items individually (as loops do). In languages that support them, they can often replace an equivalent loop with a simpler alternative.

For example, this snippet takes a set of numbers and filters out all the non-prime ones using loops.

```java
Iterator<Integer> numbersIterator -
        numbers.iterator();
Set<Integer> primeNumbers = new HashSet<>();
while (numbersIterator.hasNext()) {
    int n = numbersIterator.next();
    boolean isPrime = true;
    for (int i = 2; isPrime && i <= n / 2; i++) {
        if (n % i == 0) {
            isPrime = false;
        }
    }
    if (isPrime) {
        primeNumbers.add(n);
    }
}
```

However, you could replace this loop with a functional programming approach:

```java
public boolean isPrime(int n)
{
    return IntStream.rangeClosed(2, n / 2)
            .noneMatch(i -> n % i == 0);
}
// ...


Set<Integer> primeNumbers = numbers.stream()
        .filter(n -> isPrime(n))
        .collect(Collectors.toSet());
```

While the syntax may take a little getting used to (admittedly, functional programming looks prettier in many other languages), there's no housekeeping code, and it is conceptually easier to deal with. In this case, the isPrime function takes all integers between 2 and $\frac{n}{2}$ inclusively and verifies none of them divide cleanly into n. The set, primeNumbers, is created by filtering out everything in numbers that fails that test.

CHAPTER 6

Subroutines

Objectives

In this chapter, you'll learn:

- How subroutine size affects program comprehension
- About measures you can takc to frustrate comprehension of subroutines, specifically by
    - naming them poorly;
    - making them overly complex; and
    - giving them too many purposes
- How inputs to and outputs from subroutines can be abused

Prerequisites

It will help you if you're already familiar with reference types and value types, as well as evaluation strategies like call-by-value and call-by-reference.

Introduction

It is a very foolish and bad habit [. . .] to start working at details before having understood the problem as a whole.

—George Pólya (1973)

If you're unfortunate enough to have received training in programming, you probably learned about problem decomposition. That's where, prior to coding, you break a problem down hierarchically into smaller pieces (see Figure 6-1).

© Karl Beecher 2018
K. Beecher, *Bad Programming Practices 101*, https://doi.org/10.1007/978-1-4842-3411-2_6

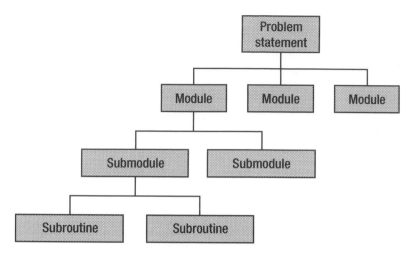

Figure 6-1. *A model of problem decomposition*

Levels in the hierarchy end up corresponding to various parts of your program. Things in the middle levels become the organizational parts of your program (like modules, classes, or packages),[1] while the lowest-level parts will describe the indivisible units of functionality the program provides. These parts of the problem correspond to subroutines in your program.

Subroutines are intended to help. You're supposed to write subroutines that correspond with those individual units of functionality. To that end, your subroutines are expected to be logical, small, and simple.

But it's not your *raison d'être* to help. By the time you get through with this chapter, you'll have learned instead how to make subroutines flabby, incoherent, and frustratingly complex.

Super-Size Your Subroutines

When Chapter 2 briefly introduced subroutines, it demonstrated the first example of the anti-rule *"In general, bigger is better."* It showed how monolithic programs tie everyone to a low-level view of the code, preventing anyone from seeing the forest for the trees. It also demonstrated how monoliths encourage something that really gets up programmers' noses: code duplication.

---

[1]These will be described in later chapters.

Because of reasons like this, the taskmaster reviewing your code may well pressure you into breaking a large program down into smaller subroutines. However, that doesn't mean you have to give up your predilection for enormous chunks of code. By investing minimal effort into creating the subroutines, you can instead break up a very large program into just a few still-rather-large subroutines.

Admittedly, this means you are replacing a monolithic piece of code with a series of subroutine calls. This raises the chance of accidentally making it easier to understand what the program is doing by allowing the reader to peruse the names of the subroutines, so keep in mind the anti-rule, *"Names are important—so make sure you get them wrong."*[2] Nevertheless, a few big subroutines can still provide a lot of trees to obscure the view.

Thumbs Down!

Experienced programmers object to large subroutines for many reasons. For example, large subroutines tend to include many details, which require a lot of effort to understand all at once. They also tend to perform more than one task, making them harder to reuse.

Large subroutines can also be harder to maintain. Making a change to one part of a subroutine risks causing knock-on effects to other parts of that subroutine, a risk that increases the larger the subroutine grows. This results in "brittle" code blocks that are resistant to change.

Also, the number of bugs in a subroutine tends to increase with size (Enders and Rombach, 2003). However, keep in mind that size is only one indicator among several, and it's actually one of the weaker ones. Just writing smaller subroutines won't *guarantee* that you've made them less buggy, but it's a good place to start, and a smaller subroutine is cheaper to fix when it does go wrong (Selby and Basili, 1991).

Coming up with a concrete number for what constitutes "too large" is tricky. The programming language used matters, empirical evidence is patchy, and the numbers found in style guides and handbooks varies. At the lower end of the advice spectrum, you find limits like 20 lines of code (Martin, 2009). At the other end, you'll find people urging you not to exceed 100 to 200 lines (McConnell, 2003), which in my own opinion is already *very* large.

---

[2]Also see the section "Make Them Hard to Understand" later in this chapter.

Put Up Barriers to Understanding

A program can be made more comprehensible overall by being restructured into a series of smaller, easily understood subroutines. This section will discuss how to neutralize that benefit by making the subroutines themselves incomprehensible.

Bad Naming

Chapter 3 explained how naming a variable sensibly risks revealing that variable's purpose, which makes things far too easy for the reader. Other things besides variables require naming, which is why we have the anti-rule *"Names are important—so make sure you get them wrong."*

Subroutines need names too, so you should reuse ideas from Chapter 3 regarding poor naming (and, yes, I know "reuse" is a dirty word in this book, but reusing *bad* ideas is okay by me). Names like f, blah, and procFshDBCnt2 are fine examples for shrouding a subroutine's purpose in secrecy, seeing as they either carry no meaning or verge on being cipher text.

If your colleagues block such poor names and insist on better ones, you could try names that are merely vague rather than incomprehensible. Labels like doProcess or runComputation are wonderfully weak because they contain no specific information.

You can also get up to mischief by giving a subroutine a name that fails to fully describe everything it does. By doing so, you can sneak unseen side effects past your colleagues. For example, someone might use your subroutine named searchInFile, which reports whether a string appears in a given file:

```
File myFile = new File(path);
if (searchInFile(myFile, "gold")) {
    // Do stuff if string found.
}
```

The programmer looking for "gold" didn't look too deep into your subroutine. However, they subsequently noticed something strange: the files they searched through sometimes suddenly went missing. After a laborious debugging session, they finally took a look at the searchInFile method:

```
boolean searchInFile(File f, String text) {
    BufferedReader br = new BufferedReader(
```

```
            new FileReader(f));
    String line;

    while ( (line = br.readLine()) != null) {
        if (line.contains(text)) {
            return true;
        }
    }

    f.delete();
    return false;
}
```

Woah there! The unsuspecting programmer has let themselves in for a world of trouble, because your humble subroutine doesn't only search for text in a file; it also *deletes* the file if the search term wasn't found. However, the subroutine's name made no mention of that.

Thumbs Down!

Poor names in the codebase generally lead to development that is lengthier and more problematic (Gorla et al., 1990). Colleagues will thank you for using subroutine names that are clear and complete. A subroutine called, say, `processNumbers` is named poorly because it's too weak. A more explicative name would be `calculateMedian`.

High Complexity

You can think of a subroutine as something that "stitches together" different blocks of code. The result can be simple or complex depending on your stitching skills.

We've already met this idea of complexity. Earlier chapters showed us how to make overly complex conditionals (Chapter 4) and write brain-bending loops (Chapter 5). Thankfully, much of the same bad advice carries over to subroutines. This shouldn't be surprising since a subroutine typically contains a mixture of things like conditionals and loops. That means, when you give a subroutine complex loops or conditionals, the subroutine suffers in turn. Go back and read those earlier chapters if you want to retread that ground.

Every time you stitch an extra loop or another conditional into a subroutine, you add more possible pathways through the subroutine, because constructs like `if` statements and `while` loops include decision points (as Figure 2-2 showed). Every pathway is another possibility you have to verify. Piling in more pathways increasingly burdens the reader's mental capacity and adds to the risk they overlook problems in your code.

This is why complexity serves as more fertile ground for growing problems than does subroutine size alone. In fact, you can write relatively small subroutines that are nevertheless overly complex. For example:

```
for (CustomerOrder order : orders) {
    vatRate = 0;
    if (order.isDomestic()) {
        vatRate += 0.15;
    } else {
        for (Country country : countries) {
            if (country.equals(order.getOrigin()) &&
                country.hasNoVatException()) {
                vatRate += country.getVatRate();
            }
        }
    }

    itemAmount = 0;
    for (Item item : order.getItems()) {
        if (item.isDiscounted()) {
            itemAmount += item.getPrice();
        }
        else {
            itemAmount += item.getDiscountedPrice();
        }
    }
    orderAmount = itemAmount * vatRate;
}
```

This subroutine is only about 15 lines long, but the number of decisions means that it has 8 pathways through it. This number actually approaches the maximum level recommended by some of those goodie-goodie authors of software best practices.

Thumbs Down!

You can code complexity using a number of means, but this book has so far focused on a simple and readily accepted one: counting the number of possible pathways through a piece of code. It actually has a name: *cyclometric complexity* (McCabe, 1976).

Calculating cyclometric complexity gives you an indication of how complex a subroutine is. To do it, begin with the number 1 (every routine has at least one pathway). From there, count each decision point in the routine. A decision point is either

- a conditional or looping construct that makes a comparison (denoted by a keyword like `if`, `while`, `for`, `case`, etc.); or

- a binary operator in an expression (like `&&` and `||`).

An instance of each adds 1 to a subroutines' cyclometric complexity. For example,

```
for (CustomerOrder order : orders)
```

adds 1, whereas

```
if (country.equals(order.getOrigin()) &&
    country.hasNoVatException())
```

adds 2, one each for the `if` and `&&`.

Your colleagues appreciate complexity's being kept low because the more decision points a subroutine contains, the more effort it takes to understand it and verify that it works as intended. The recommended upper limit varies, but typical values hover around 10 to 15 (McConnell, 2003; Watson and McCabe, 1996).

Some simple steps toward reducing a subroutine's complexity include

- simplifying the expressions in decision points;

- eliminating duplicated code within a subroutine; and

- moving one complex part of the code into its own subroutine.[3]

---

[3]That won't reduce the overall complexity, but it will help the reader who is trying to understand this particular bit of the program.

The last example could be rewritten like this:

```
for (CustomerOrder order : orders) {
    vatRate = calculateTaxRate(order);
    itemAmount = calculateOrderTotal(order.items());
    orderAmount = itemAmount * vatRate;
}
```

Some of the code has been moved into subroutines. This reduces this subroutine's own complexity to 2. The subroutines it calls each have a complexity of 5 or less.

Too Many Purposes

For surviving in the wild, which would you prefer: a single flimsy blade or a multi-purpose Swiss Army knife? In a role-playing video game, what's the better choice of character: a weakling with one skill or a kick-ass warrior with all stats cranked up across the board? Obviously, multi-talented wins every time.

Applying this same logic to subroutines leads us to conclude that the best subroutines are multi-talented and carry out lots of diverse functions. The more things a subroutine can do, the better, right?

So, let's say your task is to write code for accepting a customer order. The program needs to validate the order, print it to the screen, and store it in the database. In which case, you should write a subroutine that does all those tasks.

```
void acceptOrder(CustomerOrder order) {
    // Validate it
    if (order.getName().length() == 0 &&
        order.getItemNumber() == 0) {
        // Put up error message
    }

    // Print it
    System.out.println("Order: " + order.getId());
    System.out.println("Name: " + order.getName());
    System.out.println("Items:");
    for (OrderItem item : order.getItems()) {
        System.out.println(" - " + item);
    }
```

```
    // Save it
    DbConnection conn = openDbConnection();
    conn.saveOrder(order);
    conn.close();
}
```

Because it can do everything, `acceptOrder` is a Swiss Army knife, a multi-skilled video-game character. That makes it better.

Right?

Thumbs Down!

No. A subroutine should focus on a single task.

The main problem with `acceptOrder` stems from its being an "all or nothing" subroutine. Your program can either validate, print, and save a customer's order all together or do none of those things. What if more granular control were needed? What if the program sometimes needed to accept an order silently, without printing it to the screen? What if it occasionally needed to validate and print an order, but store it temporarily on disk instead of in the database? The current version of `acceptOrder` doesn't allow for any of that. This multi-purpose subroutine imposes a rigid order on proceedings.

You have various options to handle this. Among the least acceptable approaches would be to add tweaked copies of the original subroutine (e.g., `acceptOrderSilently` and `acceptOrderStoreToDisk`). Expect this solution to be rejected for excessive code duplication.

A more acceptable solution might be to keep `acceptOrder` multi-purpose, but add parameters allowing the caller to control the behavior. For example:

```
void acceptOrder(CustomerOrder order,
      boolean printOrder) {
   // Validate it
   if (order.getName().length() > 0 &&
       order.getItemNumber() > 0) {
      // Put up error message
   }
```

```
    // Print it
    if (printOrder) {
        System.out.println("Order: " + order.getId());
        // etc...
```

Better still would be to extract each individual task into its own subroutine:

```
boolean isValid(CustomerOrder order) {
    return order.getName().length() > 0 &&
        order.getItemNumber() > 0;
}

void printOrder(CustomerOrder order) {
    System.out.println("Order: " + order.getId());
    System.out.println("Name: " + order.getName());
    System.out.println("Items:");
    for (OrderItem item : order.getItems()) {
        System.out.println(" - " + item);
    }
}

void saveOrderToDb(CustomerOrder order) {
    DbConnection conn = openDbConnection();
    conn.saveOrder(order);
    conn.close();
}
```

That would give you the option of adding new use cases in the future by simply combining the simpler subroutines in different ways as necessary.

If anything should be flexible and multi-purpose it should be the program, not its individual subroutines. Think of the program as the Swiss Army knife and the subroutines—each finely attuned for a single purpose—as the individual blades.

(Ab)use Parameters

Subroutines need information to work with. The preferred way to supply it is via parameters. But just because it's preferable, that doesn't mean it isn't open to abuse.

The More the Merrier

If you have a procedure with ten parameters, you probably missed some.

—Alan Perlis (1982)

Concerning the number of parameters a subroutine should accept, other people on your project probably toe the usual line, which advises keeping the number small—only up to about two or three, in fact. Your colleagues will expect you to do the same and might even point out a few examples like these:

```
boolean isOldEnough = isAdult(age);
String name = germanName.replace("ß", "ss");
```

They might also harp on about how keeping parameter lists small helps keep subroutines small and focused and all that sort of thing. But such colleagues misunderstand your mission. You don't play by their rules. You play by anti-rules, ones like *"The bigger the better."* That's why you prefer big parameter lists.

```
void processCustomer(String forename,
        int age, List<Order> orders,
        String phoneNumber, String surname,
        Date dateOfBirth, String mothersMaidenName,
        boolean marketingEmails)
```

Imagine, if you can bear it, being a colleague faced with this code and the questions that would go through their mind. What on earth is this subroutine's purpose?[4] How much work does it do if it requires all those parameters? Are they all strictly necessary? And why are they in that order?

Thumbs Down!

A couple of very common reasons for parameter lists' growing too long are as follows:

1. The subroutine is trying to do too much.

2. Most or all of the parameters would make more sense being unified into a new type.[5]

---

[4]We've cunningly reused the bad naming strategy from the earlier section "Put Up Barriers to Understanding."

[5]Chapter 9 will discuss custom types in more detail.

Regarding the first reason, this chapter already discussed in an earlier section how to handle subroutines' doing too much (see "Put Up Barriers to Understanding").

Regarding the second reason, let's assume as an example that `processCustomer` has just one task, say, adding a new customer to the system. Yes, that requires several pieces of information, but see how much you can simplify the subroutine by gathering all those pieces together into a single, new type:

```
// We created this new class...
class Customer {
    String forename;
    String surname;
    Date dateOfBirth;
    String mothersMaidenName;
    boolean sendMarketingEmails;
    List<Order> orders;
}

// ...


// ... and replaced all the old parameters.
void addNewCustomer(Customer newCustomer)
```

Being Defensive

Defensive is not a word associated with winners. Winners never get defensive, as they always prefer the offensive. That's true of all the great names from history: Caesar, Napoleon, Patton, Stone Cold Steve Austin. That's why whenever anyone suggests writing subroutines defensively, you should treat them like the loser they clearly are.

A subroutine written defensively takes precautions against potentially problematic parameters. Look at this, for example:

```
void shoutMessage(String message) {
    // WINNERS SHOUT. To shout a message, turn the
    // whole thing to upper-case.
    System.out.println(message.toUpperCase());
}
```

Your colleagues will urge caution against using the `message` parameter without checking it. But losers are cautious. After all, did Caesar hesitate when the soothsayer cautioned him to beware the Ides of March? No, he fearlessly marched into the Senate without a bodyguard. (Admittedly, he then got stabbed to death, but that's beside the point.)

Instead, you should follow the anti-rule, *"Assume nothing will go wrong."* Your boldness will be rewarded. See what glory awaits you when the program is run:

```
Exception in thread "main" java.lang.NullPointerException
        at Main.shoutMessage(Main.java:16)
        at Main.main(Main.java:10)
```

Oh. Um . . . I guess `shoutMessage` was called with `null` as the parameter.

Which leads onto the next lesson: winners know exactly when to walk away exclaiming, "Too bad, but it's not my problem!"

Thumbs Down!

A significant proportion of errors occur at the boundaries between subroutines (Basili and Perricone, 1984). Invalid data's crossing those boundaries can cause errors. Therefore, parameters should always be checked before use.

Simple checking[6] usually adds just a few extra lines of code. A safer version of `shoutMessage` would look like this:

```
void shoutMessage(String message) {
    if (message != null) {
        System.out.println(message.toUpperCase());
    }
}
```

Examples of checking parameters include the following:

- Ensuring objects are non-null before trying to call their methods

- Verifying numerical values are within expected mathematical bounds (e.g., divisors shouldn't be zero, square roots shouldn't be taken of a negative number)

---

[6]Chapter 7 will discuss more-sophisticated error-handling techniques.

- Checking that specially formatted data conforms to the expected format (e.g., dates, times, credit card numbers)

- Making sure files are open and readable before trying to access them

Surreptitious Subroutines

People like surprises. That's why it's a good idea to make your programs do unexpected things.

When it comes to parameters, a great way to cause surprise (not to mention consternation) is to make your subroutines alter parameter values when that's not expected. A programmer faced with a method like this:

```
void addCustomerToList(Customer c,
        List<Customer> customers)
```

can reasonably expect that calling addCustomerToList will change the contents of the customers argument. However, they would expect that same list to remain unchanged after calling a method like this:

```
void outputList(List<Customer> customers)
```

Conscious of these sorts of expectations, you should learn to sneak surprising and unwanted side effects into your subroutines. Here's a small example.

A DisplayBoard is an announcement screen like you might find in a train station. You can keep adding messages to the board until you run out of space (the board is limited to a maximum of 280 characters). You can check that your message fits before adding it, like this:

```
if (displayBoard.fits(message)) {
    displayBoard.add(message);
}
```

Here's the first part of the DisplayBoard code, including only its data fields:

```
class DisplayBoard {
    // This is what gets displayed
    StringBuilder text;

    // etc.
```

Here's the add method:

```
public void add(String message) {
    text.append(message);
}
```

Nothing surprising there. Here's the fits method:

```
public boolean fits(String message) {
    return text.append(message).length() <= 280;
}
```

Ah, here we have a problem—one which might well be overlooked in review.

The fits method doesn't just perform a check (as expected); it also performs a *change*. It doesn't just simulate what the updated message's length would be, it actually adds the new message to the board then returns whether or not the whole text has a length of less than or equal to 280 characters. Therefore, checking to see if a message fits before adding it to the board results in its appearing on the board twice!

Screw with Return Values

As well as accepting values, subroutines can also return them. As with parameters, there are certain things your colleagues would prefer you not do.

Here are some of them.

Return of the Harbinger

As Chapter 3 pointed out,[7] null values can be dangerous, as they have the potential to kill a program quicker than you can say "null pointer exception." Chapter 3 gave an example where return values from a subroutine were used without first verifying they were non-null, thus planting seeds from which should eventually bloom an error.

Now that we're addressing the other side of the boundary between caller and receiver, we can revisit this case. Suffice it to say, you can also encourage bugs from the receiver side, where the author decides what gets returned. Sure, you will have to return a real object at some point, but many languages allow you to return from a subroutine

---

[7]In the section "Null—The Harbinger of Doom."

at multiple points. Therefore, sprinkling around plenty of `return null` statements is a good start. For example, a subroutine that returns a collection could return null if there's nothing to put into the collection, or a subroutine could return null if it encounters an error.

In short: if in doubt, return null.

Thumbs Down!

There's sometimes a better alternative to returning nulls from a subroutine; for example:

- A subroutine that returns a collection could return an empty collection instead of null.

- A subroutine that encounters a problem could (and should) throw an exception.

- If you return a custom type, it sometimes makes sense to have the idea of a default value for that type rather than null, similar to the idea of an empty string or a default date.

Some languages have stronger null safety built-in. They force the programmer to specify whether a variable is nullable and will refuse to even compile a program until every reference to a nullable return value includes code handling a null return.

Java isn't one of these languages. However, as Chapter 3 explained, it does provide the `Optional` type, which makes it clear that an object may or may not be null and forces the caller of the subroutine to take that into account. However, since the language doesn't force you to use it, the use of `Optional` is itself optional.

Fun with Output Parameters

Subroutines that alter parameter values can make for some wonderful confusion. Take a look at this example, a simple subroutine that moves a pair of *x-y* coordinates:

```java
void move(int x, int xDistance,
        int y, int yDistance) {
    x = x + xDistance;
    y = y + yDistance;
}
```

A typical call to move would look like this:

```
move(x, 10, y, -20);
```

Nothing surprising there. Compare it to another subroutine that keeps a history of all the movements made:

```
void recordMovement(int x, List<Integer> xs,
        int y, List<Integer> ys) {
    xs.add(x);
    ys.add(y);
}
```

Again, pretty straightforward. So, think about what the output of this code would be:

```
int xPos = 5;
int yPos = 5;
List<Integer> xMoves = new ArrayList<>();
List<Integer> yMoves = new ArrayList<>();

System.out.println("X: " + xPos + ", Y: " + yPos);

move(xPos, 10, yPos, -20);
recordMovement(10, xMoves, -20, yMoves);

System.out.println("X-Movements: " + xMoves);
System.out.println("Y-Movements: " + yMoves);
System.out.println("X: " + xPos + ", Y: " + yPos);
```

What will the program output look like? What will appear in place of the following question marks?

```
X: ?, Y: ?
X-Movements: ?
Y-Movements: ?
X: ?, Y: ?
```

Thumbs Down!

Here's the correct answer.

```
X: 5, Y: 5
X-Movements: [10]
Y-Movements: [-20]
X: 5, Y: 5
```

Notice how the values of xPos and yPos didn't change, but xMoves and yMoves did? If you guessed differently, chances are Java's evaluation strategy caught you out.

The evaluation strategy describes exactly what is sent to a subroutine when arguments are passed in a call. Different languages use different strategies, so you must learn which strategy your chosen language applies. Java always uses call-by-value, which means the *value* of the argument (rather than the argument itself) is copied into a new, local variable (i.e., the parameter). The original variable can't be altered by the subroutine. However, Java's type system (which divides all types into primitive and reference types) throws up some complications.

A primitive type (like int) stores the variable's actual value. In the middle of calling the move method, there are two variables, xPos and x, and x is local to move.

```java
void move(int x, int xDistance,
        int y, int yDistance) {
    // x=5, y=5, xDistance=10, yDistance=-20
    x = x + xDistance;
    // At this point, x=15 and xPos=5
    y = y + yDistance;
}
```

That's why executing the statement x = x + xDistance in the move method does nothing to alter the original value of xPos. It only alters the local parameter. That's why xPos (and yPos) remained 5, even after the move method completed.

A reference type (like ArrayList) stores an object's location in memory. Therefore, passing a reference type to a method means that the object's memory location is copied to the corresponding parameter. That means the variable xMoves and the parameter xs are two different labels but they point to the same single object.

```
void recordMovement(int x, List<Integer> xs,
        int y, List<Integer> ys) {
    // x=10, xs=[], xMovements=[]
    xs.add(x);
    // At this point, xs=[10], xMovements=[10]
    ys.add(y);
}
```

Calling a mutator method on such a parameter sends a message to the original object to change itself. That's why, in our example, the changes made by executing xs.add(x) remained visible after the move method completed.

In the example, the author intended to use output parameters, which are parameters passed to subroutines simply to have their values altered.

- In the case of the recordMovements method, xMoves and yMoves were output parameters.

- In the case of move, xPos and yPos were intended to be output parameters, but Java's evaluation strategy prevented that.

There's nothing *inherently* wrong with using output parameters—they have their place—but they're often discouraged today as being confusing and awkward to use. Keep in mind your colleagues' desire for consistency throughout the codebase, and also that a stronger preference for using immutable types[8] is emerging these days, which disfavors output parameters.

In short, my advice is this: if a subroutine must update a variable, prefer creating a new value based on input parameters and return it, rather than using output parameters. Make output parameters an exception when they can be justified.

---

[8]The value of an immutable type can't be altered once it's been set.

CHAPTER 7

Error Handling

Objectives

In this chapter, you'll learn:

- Typical error-handling techniques and how to ignore them

- How to suppress errors

- How to dodge responsibility for handling errors altogether

- How to make error-handling as messy an affair as possible

Prerequisites

Before reading this chapter, it will help if you're familiar with:

- Assertions

- Exceptions, including some of the most common exception types in Java (e.g., `NullPointerException`, `IOException`)

- Stack traces

Introduction

Any man can make mistakes, but only a fool persists in his error.

—Cicero

As if you couldn't guess, making a mess of error-handling is a great way to cause problems in a program. This chapter will discuss various ways of giving bugs the space they need to flourish.

© Karl Beecher 2018
K. Beecher, *Bad Programming Practices 101*, https://doi.org/10.1007/978-1-4842-3411-2_7

Assume Everything Will Always Go Well

Common advice from programming elders is to assume the worst when writing code. "Things always threaten to go wrong," the "wise" ones will say, "so program in a way that anticipates errors at any moment." Poor devils. They may be more experienced, but they've allowed their experience to turn them into paranoiacs who live constantly in fear of bugs.

So much can go wrong during the execution of a program, the only teacher who has sensible advice is the ostrich: when trouble brews, just stick your head in the sand and ignore it. It's the key to a happy life, if not to stable software.

Don't Check

Chapter 6 already talked about being cautious[1] and how such behavior is for losers. Checking inputs before you process them might seem innocuous, but it's actually the gateway to paranoia. Don't do it. Otherwise, before you know it, you'll be writing documentation, adhering to standards, and using bug databases (*ugh!*). Once that happens, no hope remains for you.

An example of defensive programming is verifying that an input has an expected value before attempting to manipulate it, like this:

```
if (message != null) {
    System.out.println(message.toUpperCase());
}
```

Obviously, you should avoid this form, but you should also watch out for defensive programming, which has other manifestations. Some programming constructs offer methods for you to deal with unanticipated outcomes. For example, the `switch` statement often has an optional `default` clause in many languages. The code in a `default` block gets executed when the value of the tested expression matches none of the `case` values.

```
String drinkOrder = getNextOrder();

// Maps drinks to prices (in cents)
Map<String, Integer> invoice = getCurrentInvoice();
```

---

[1]See the subsection "Being Defensive."

```java
switch (drinkOrder) {
    case "Cappuccino":
        invoice.put(drinkOrder, 399);
        break;
    case "Latte":
        invoice.put(drinkOrder, 449);
        break;
    case "Mocha":
        invoice.put(drinkOrder, 499);
        break;
    default:
        System.out.println("Unknown drink: " +
                drinkOrder);
        break;
}
```

In this example, the program matches drinks to prices. If the program doesn't recognize a drink (an unlikely but nevertheless possible unanticipated outcome), it can't process the drink's price, and the user needs alerting of that fact.

Thus, the default clause is a kind of catch-all for miscellaneous or unanticipated outcomes. Suffice it to say, the default clause is a way to sneak in paranoid code that can catch potential problems. Using it is another way those defensive coders try to get you.

Don't Assert

There's actually no shortage of ways defensive programmers try to get to you. They offer you tools and techniques like they're candy, imploring you to "try it and see if you like it."

Just say no. Otherwise, before you know it, you'll be hooked.

A particularly powerful tool on offer is assertions, which many programming languages have in some form. An assertion is a statement you can put into a program at a specific point that tests whether a certain condition is true or not. If the condition is true, no further action is taken, but if it's not, the program typically terminates immediately.[2] Here's an example:

```
void getTemperatureInKelvin() {
    // Gets a reading in Celsius.
    double temperatureC = getReading();

    // Converts to degrees Kelvin
    temperatureK = temperatureC + 273.15;

    assert temperatureK >= 0 : "Invalid temperature!";
}
```

Since zero degrees Kelvin is absolute zero (and a lower temperature is a physical impossibility), ending up with a negative value for the temperature in degrees Kelvin means something has gone very wrong.

Pushers of assertions will sell them to you using seductive arguments. "Look," they'll say, "see how useful they are . . ." Other arguments include:

- An easy way to verify your assumptions.

- So quick to write. Just a single line of code.

- You're not forced to use them. In fact, assertions are turned off by default. You have to activate them for assertions to have any effect.[3]

Naturally, the only acceptable way to use assertions (outside of avoiding them entirely) is to *misuse* them.

One way to misuse them is to apply them as your exclusive means of error-handling. This takes advantage of their simple binary nature. Either everything is hunky-dory (and the program continues) or something is wrong, causing the program to crash in flames, even if the error is only of the slightest severity. Also, since assertions are typically turned off by default, error-checking done by assertions may as well not exist under normal conditions.

---

[2]In Java, this works by throwing an AssertionError object.
[3]In Java, do this by running the program with the -ea argument.

Another way to misuse assertions is to execute state-changing operations inside the assert statement. Look at this:

```
void haveBirthday() {
    // This method increases age by 1.
    assert (age++ > 0) : "Invalid age!";
}
```

This code increases age by 1, simulating a birthday. The actual functionality, age++ (which is the same as saying age = age + 1), is combined with the assertion. This cleverly saves a line of code, but also makes sure that the program behaves correctly only when assertions are turned on.

Thumbs Down!

The standard use of assertions is to make clear your assumptions and catch any impossible situations. (Less severe types of problems can be dealt with more subtly using exception handling—see next section.) Assertions often take the form of either a precondition (something that must be true before an operation can take place) or a postcondition (which must be true after an operation takes place). The getTemperatureInKelvin subroutine is an example of a postcondition because it verifies that the calculation has produced a valid result.

Assertions are typically turned on only during development and testing. They're rarely kept active once a program has been released. That's why the haveBirthday example is particularly problematic: there's a chance that the code works fine during development, but stops working as expected once the program has gone into production.

Checking an assertion shouldn't cause a change in state. A better way to write the haveBirthday method would have been like this:

```
void haveBirthday() {
    age = age + 1;

    // Postcondition: Age must be greater than zero
    // after having a birthday.
    assert (age > 0) : "Invalid age!";
}
```

This way, haveBirthday functions whether assertions are active or not.

Don't Catch

This section began by recommending the ostrich strategy. Here's where that approach can really pay off.

Programming languages typically have features allowing you to specify what to do in case of a problem. Many of today's popular languages provide such a feature in the form of exception handling. In Java, potentially problematic code is isolated in a `try` block, and problems that arise are dealt with in the corresponding `catch` block.

The great thing about exceptions is that catching them is optional. And, as the first anti-rule of programming says, "*Something that is not mandatory is not worth doing.*" So, by ignoring the danger, you guarantee that any exception raised gets thrown back at the calling code for someone else to worry about. With luck, that exception never gets caught and causes the program to crash.

Thumbs Down!

Ignoring exceptions is simply dangerous.

An exception tells you a piece of code is unable to do the job expected of it. This is information you need to know because it gives you an opportunity to rescue the program from failure. After all, if a program attempts to open a file using a user-provided name, what's the reasonable thing to do if the file can't be found? Crash horribly? Or recognize that a problem occurred and ask the user to input the name again?

Our example language, Java, takes things a little further than other languages by distinguishing between checked and unchecked exceptions.[4] Every exception in Java is either one or the other:

- Unchecked exceptions are intended for serious programming errors considered irrevocable (ESA, 2004). These can optionally be ignored.

- Checked exceptions are intended for problems that, while rare, nevertheless can happen under normal operation (ESA, 2004). They *can't* be ignored, and they form part of a method's signature.

For example, consider this method:

```
File getConfigFile() throws IOException
```

---

[4]Admittedly, this feature is far from universally loved.

An `IOException` is a checked exception. Therefore, if you call this method you don't have the option of ignoring the potential exception. You must enclose the calling code in an appropriate `try` block.

What to do inside a `try` block is discussed in the following section.

Send Problems Down the Memory Hole

. . . he crumpled up the original message and any notes that he himself had made, and dropped them into the memory hole to be devoured by the flames.

— George Orwell, *Nineteen Eighty-Four* (1949)

Ignoring potential problems may only get you so far. Eventually, your colleagues may, shall we say, *compel* you to recognize that problems can occur in programs and that you should take precautions to handle them. What then are your options?

You don't want to do effective error-handling, obviously, so you should put ineffective error-handling in place, treating exceptions as unworthy of attention, inconvenient facts that—once identified—ought to be ignored, suppressed, and sent down the memory hole.

Disappearing Exceptions

The previous section advised you to ignore exceptions completely. However, finger-wagging colleagues and overzealous programming languages can conspire to prevent you from doing so. In the end, you might have no choice but to include an error-handling block.

Thankfully, there's more than one way to ignore an exception. If you're forced to include a `try` block, then simply subvert the whole structure. Just because you catch something doesn't mean you have to do anything with it. Why not just silently drop it?

Look at this example. An application allows a user to set custom settings. It stores that configuration in a file. Every time the application loads, it opens the file, reads the contents, and customizes the environment according to the user's settings.

```
// Gets the file location of the application's
// configuration information
File configFile = new File(configFileLocation);
```

```
try {
    parseConfigFile(configFile);
    // Code for adjusting app to config settings goes
    // here...
}
catch (FileNotFoundException e) {
    // Leave this empty. Do nothing.
}
```

Of course, things can go wrong; for instance, the configuration file could go missing. In this case, the application would still function, but it would do so without the user's custom settings. The effect runs two-fold:

1. The user sees their custom settings have gone missing, but for no good reason. Nothing appeared to explain to them what happened.

2. By silently dropping the exception, you leave behind no clue to help the programmer determine the problem in case the user complains (as they are apt to do).

Reporting Problems Is Doubleplusungood

A simple and unobtrusive way to deal with problems is to report them. But who wants to be the bearer of bad news? Not you.

However, if your hand is forced and you're compelled to add some kind of error reporting, you can nevertheless report problems without the risk of being helpful.

You might be told to make the program write messages when something goes wrong. So be it, but make sure you do so as invisibly as possible. For example, if your program is a graphical application, report problems using the standard print statement (like System.out.println) because those messages are sent to the console and will probably go unseen.

Failing this, you might be forced to display prominent messages to the user when a problem occurs. In this situation, it's best to bamboozle the user with inappropriately technical and complicated information. A message with jargon, error codes, and a stack trace is a good candidate (see Figure 7-1).

Figure 7-1. *An example of a bad error message*

Better the user is confused than informed.

Thumbs Down!

When you report a problem, the location and content of the report depends on the audience.

An error message for the user should take into account the user's technical aptitude. Unless you have a good reason to assume otherwise, you should imagine the user to be a non-programmer. Stack traces and error codes won't help them; you should explain in clear, non-technical language what went wrong and what (if anything) can be done about it. For example:

```
File configFile = new File(configFileLocation);

try {
    parseConfigFile(configFile);
}
catch (FileNotFoundException e) {
    // Give helpful, non-technical information to
    // the user in a dialog window.
```

```
Alert alert = new Alert(AlertType.ERROR);
alert.setTitle("Configuration problem");
alert.setHeaderText("Configuration information was lost or corrupted.");
alert.setContentText("The application will continue to run with default
settings. Please contact your system administrator.");
alert.show();
}
```

A message like that in Figure 7-2 will pop-up to the user.

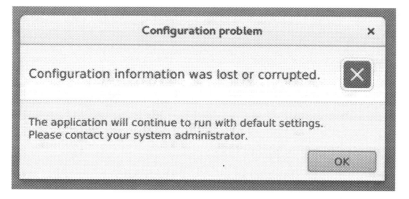

Figure 7-2. *An example of a more informative error message*

Heavily technical information is useful, but only for the program's author. That information should be stored in the program's log for later retrieval when the programmer comes to diagnosing the problem. That means writing messages to a file, not printing them to the console, where they go unrecorded and possibly even unseen. Most programming languages provide their own standard logging functions for this.[5]

Kick the Can Down the Road

Every problem eventually has to be dealt with by somebody. And preferably somebody *else*. You can make sure of that by adopting a policy of passing problems onto other areas of the program, ones that are the responsibility of other people.

---

[5]Logging will be discussed in more detail in Chapter 10, "Debugging."

In other words, kick the can down the road, preferably hard and in a way that's likely to hurt someone.

Using Error Codes

So, all that previous, sensible advice about dealing with exceptions locally if possible goes out the window. When a problem arises, your code is going to reflexively pass the buck. The question then remains: in what manner should you pass it?

If you can, you should choose a method that's as uninformative as possible so the receiver of the buck learns little or nothing about the problem. You should also choose a method that passes the buck along so quietly that it can easily be missed.

In most languages, error statuses and error codes can be misused to fit these requirements nicely. We met error codes already in Chapter 3,[6] which also pointed out that exceptions are generally preferred over error codes. Naturally, that should be enough to persuade you to prefer error codes. If you need more persuasion, consider some of their delightful drawbacks:

- Returning an error code forces the caller to deal with an error in one specific place: the place from which they called your subroutine.

- When new error codes are added, this can mean a program requires recompilation and redeployment. For example, error codes in Java are normally kept in an enum, which is used throughout the system. The effects of updating this enum cascade to other classes in the program far and wide.

As limiting as error codes can be, there's an even more uninformative alternative: the error flag. A subroutine with a Boolean return type (which holds false in the case that something went wrong) is delightfully simple and wonderfully vague.

```
boolean succeeded = parseXmlFile(myXmlFile);
if (succeeded) {
    // Do normal business
}
else {
    errorPopup("Parse failed. Don't ask why, because I don't know.");
}
```

---

[6]See the section, "Thoroughly Abuse the Type System."

What went wrong in this case? Was the file missing? Did we have insufficient access? Was the XML malformed? The caller simply doesn't know, and so they're prevented from taking any informed action.

Perhaps the best problem you cause in either case—whether your subroutine returns a code or a flag—is that the return values can be ignored, or even missed altogether (an easy mistake to make).

Thumbs Down!

Many textbooks and standards documents recommend exceptions over error codes (ESA, 2004; Martin, 2009). Some sources even say you shouldn't use error codes at all, precisely because they can be ignored (Microsoft, 2017).

Whatever approach you choose, make sure you understand the key differences:

- When the caller ignores a subroutine's error code, that code simply "disappears."

- When the caller ignores an exception, the exception persists, and it propagates back down the call stack until caught. If it's never caught, the program crashes.

This is part of what makes exceptions more powerful than error codes. Ignoring an exception might allow you to pass the problem along to be processed at a more appropriate level, but ignoring it *completely* will not make it go away.

Baffle and Bamboozle

If you lose the fight against exceptions, all is not lost. You could still use exceptions, but in a way that neutralizes some of their advantages, specifically their capacity to be informative. This can leave the caller baffled and bamboozled when they try to handle the exception.

Exceptions allow you to attach additional information, like custom messages. But—keeping in mind our anti-rule that *"Anything that isn't mandatory isn't worth doing"*—why bother, especially if it's not your code handling the problem. For example, an IOException can be raised when having trouble using an I/O device, but I/O devices are notoriously troublesome, and the root cause could be one of a thousand possible problems.

```
throw new IOException();
```

Throwing an exception like this when, say, trying to use a network connection tells the caller only that a problem occurred, but imagine being the poor sap who has to figure out how to react. What exactly was the problem? Was the network unavailable? Was it available but refused access? Was the URI not found?

Or how about this:

```
throw new IllegalArgumentException();
```

If your method accepts multiple arguments, then the caller can do little more than guess which one was problematic.

When you think about it, you're probably being too helpful when you use specifically typed exceptions like `NullPointerException`, `IOException`, or `IllegalArgumentException`. Besides which, choosing between all the different types probably soaks up too much of your precious time. Instead, just use the root `Exception` class for all problems. Quite the time-saver for you.

Thumbs Down!

When an error occurs, the programmer needs to know key information in order to diagnose it. You colleagues count on you to provide it. That comes partly from helpful error messages.

```
void assignGrade(Student student, int score)
        throws IllegalArgumentException {
    if (score < 0 || score > 100)
    {
        throw new IllegalArgumentException(
            "Score (" + score +
            ") not in acceptable range (0 to 100).";
        );
    }
    // etc...
```

119

It also comes from appropriately typed exceptions. For example, when trying to access a resource over a network, it helps to throw a type that fits the situation rather than just plain old Exception.

```
ServerResponse response = getNetworkResource(url);

if (response.getCode().equals("400")) {
    // Code 400 means URL was invalid.
    // Caller probably needs to stop and
    // inform the user.
    throw new URIException("Tried to access an" +
            " invalid URL: " + url);
}

if (response.getCode().equals("403")) {
    // Code 403 means access denied.
    // Caller might want to ask the user to
    // enter name and password and then try
    // again to connect.
    throw new AuthenticationException("Access to " +
            url + " denied.");
}
```

That way, the caller has the option to react in different ways to different problems.

Perhaps the most important thing to ask when handling an exception is: should this code throw an exception at all? Most advice will tell you that if an exception can be handled locally, then it should be. Do everything possible to avoid kicking the can down the road.

Make a Mess

Programs live in a world of their own: a sterile, mathematical world where everything is clean and orderly. The real world, however, is messy and disordered. Errors and exceptions result when these two worlds collide.

Which sounds like the perfect excuse for making error-handling a messy, disordered business.

Cleaning Up and How Not to Do It

Resources live in the real world. They include things like memory, files, networks, and databases. They make computers useful, able to do things like communicate, store information, and display things.

Now, it's bad enough that resources cause complications even under normal conditions. Being finite in nature, resources require careful management: memory space can't be exceeded, files shouldn't be written to simultaneously, databases require users to be authenticated.

But things can get *really* complicated when you account for the fact that things can go wrong and you need to add error-handling into the mix. Files can disappear unexpectedly, databases can refuse access, and networks have a habit of dying just when you need them most. When things go wrong, your program's careful management of resources can get thrown out of whack.

Everyone on your project should watch resource-handling code carefully, making sure that resources are properly cleaned up, even in the event of problems. Everyone except you, that is. You'll be taking advantage of the fact that proper resource management is hard, enabling you to slip in a few easily missed bugs here and there.

Let's take database connections as an example. A database typically runs as a separate program to which your program must connect in order to access data. It can sustain only a limited number of connections, so each connection must be closed after use.

```
DbConnection connection =
        database.getConnection(username, password);
ResultSet results = connection.runQuery(
        "SELECT * FROM User WHERE id = " + id);
connection.close();
```

If a connection is accidentally left open after use, it remains unavailable to everyone else. Forgetting to include cleanup code (like the call to the close method) is easy enough, but getting it wrong under normal conditions is fairly straightforward: either the cleanup code is missing or not.

However, bringing error-handling into it only makes it more complicated and allows you to be wrong in all sorts of other ways.

Accessing a database can go wrong in a number of ways. The connection could be lost, the query could be invalid, authorization might fail, etc. Like a conscientious programmer, you add exception-handling code for such cases:

```
try {
    DbConnection connection =
            database.getConnection(username, password);
    results = connection.runQuery(
            "SELECT * FROM User WHERE id = " + id);
    connection.close();
}
catch (ConnectionException e) {
    // Thrown if a connection fails
}
catch (QueryException e) {
    // Thrown if a query fails
}
// etc...
```

And in doing so, you add a bug to the code. Why? Because if an exception is thrown before the `connection.close()` instruction is reached, the connection will remain open.

Thumbs Down!

You must always clean up resources after use. Since things can go wrong before you get a chance to clean up, use some kind of method that takes account of that.

In most exception-supporting languages, the try block includes a `finally` clause. Code inside this block is run regardless of whether or not an exception occurred.[7]

```
try {
    DbConnection connection =
            database.getConnection(username, password);
    // do stuff with the connection...
}
```

---

[7]The `finally` block will even execute if you include a `return` statement in the try block.

```
catch (ConnectionException e) {
    // Thrown if a connection fails
}
catch (QueryException e) {
    // Thrown if a query fails
}
finally {
    connection.close();
}
```

Even better, if your chosen language can automate the cleaning up of resources, then you can use that. This way, you don't need to remember to include the code yourself. Since version 1.7, Java has included the try-with block for this purpose.

```
// DbConnection implements the java.io.AutoCloseable
// interface, so this connection will be automatically
// closed after this try-block exits.
try (DbConnection connection =
        database.getConnection(username, password)) {
    results = connection.runQuery(
            "SELECT * FROM User WHERE id = " + id);
}
catch (QueryException e) {
    // Thrown if a query fails
}
```

A try-with block differs from a try block by accepting a resource in parentheses after the try keyword (in this example, the connection object). This gives responsibility for closing the resource to the block.

CHAPTER 8

Modules

Objectives

In this chapter, you'll learn:

- How to make a mess of importing modules

- How to write modules that are hard to use and error-prone, specifically modules

  - that are inflexible, do too much, and fight against being reused; and

  - whose poor design make errors more likely and cause pain for future maintainers.

Prerequisites

Before reading this chapter, it will help if you're familiar with the following:

- The basic idea of modules and how they can be used by each other

- Access modifiers in Java (`private`, `public` etc.)

- The concept of a software interface

Introduction

Modules are supposed to help you in various ways.

For one thing, they're supposed to help you better manage complexity as a software program grows. Breaking a large program into small, clean pieces makes it easier to focus on a specific part of the program.

© Karl Beecher 2018
K. Beecher, *Bad Programming Practices 101*, https://doi.org/10.1007/978-1-4842-3411-2_8

Modules should also make a project more flexible. When a program is made up of independent components, the software becomes easier to grow, maintain, and reuse.

If reading about such benefits is starting to make you feel sick, don't worry. This chapter will show you how to write modules in a way that neuters their helpfulness.

A Note on Terminology

The term *module* is a fairly flexible one in programming. In fact, it can mean different things in different languages, sometimes having a very specific meaning.

While this book uses Java as a demonstration language, it doesn't assume any specific meaning of *module*.[1] Rather, it uses the term in a general sense that can be applied to any programming language. Thus, the principles described here could be applied to such units as functions, methods, classes, or packages.

For the purposes of this book, we'll understand a module to be a unit of code that

- is self-contained;

- is interchangeable, operating only via an interface that encapsulates the module's data; and

- focuses on a coherent, well-defined function.

Make Importing Messy

You chose this book to learn how to do things badly. That says something about you.

For example, if you ever perform home improvement or a similar form of manual labor (and I know that's a big *if*), no doubt you're the sort of utter hooligan who empties out the entire contents of the toolbox onto the floor and then scrabbles around the pile seeking the implement you need. No careful tool selection for you.

This section explores the programmatic equivalent of dumping your tools onto the floor.

---

[1] Only recently did Java apply a definitive meaning to the term upon the release of its module system with Java 9 (Oracle, 2017).

Import All the Things!

In order to use a module in your code, you typically have to import it first. Some languages allow you to choose only parts of a module to import. In these cases, the typical advice tells you to import only the specific parts you need, like picking out the one right tool from an immaculately kept toolbox.

```
import java.awt.Button
import java.awt.Canvas;
import java.awt.Paint;
// and so on and so on and so on...
```

But why bother? That just leads to more typing. Besides which, you might need something else from the same module in the future. You could instead import a module's *entire* contents as a precaution against having to do more typing. Therefore, a wildcard import makes things much easier for you.

```
// Import everything from the AWT root package.
import java.awt.*;
```

Who could possibly object to that?

Thumbs Down!

A wildcard import is hardly the world's worst programming practice. In fact, some of your colleagues might wave it through without comment. But you should be aware that some people may object to it.

One objection could be that importing everything from a module soaks up resources unnecessarily if most of the imported stuff goes unused. However, this depends on the language being used.[2]

A more general objection could be that a wildcard import can unwittingly set up name clashes. For example, in the younger days of Java (around version 1.1) a typical GUI program might have included the following imports:

```
import java.awt.*;
import java.util.*;
```

---

[2]For example, I understand wildcard import has very little effect on performance in Java.

```
// Available meals
private List meals = new List();
meals.add("Egg and Mushrooms");
meals.add("Steak and Ale Pie");
meals.add("Omelette");

// etc.
```

In this case, a List could only refer to the GUI component[3] that belonged to the java.awt package. However, after later upgrading to Java 1.2, that same program code would have suddenly thrown compile errors. This actually happened to many people. Why? Because another List was introduced to the Java Standard Library in version 1.2, namely the List interface. It was added to the java.util package, causing that reference to List in the preceding code to became ambiguous. The compiler didn't know whether you meant a java.util.List or a java.awt.List.

For reasons like this, numerous style guides require that you use explicit import statements instead of wildcards (for example, see ESA, 2004; Google, 2017b).

Clutter and Mess

If you thought the preoccupation with wildcard imports was obsessive, wait until you see this. If only for your own amusement, see what reactions you can provoke among colleagues by adding import statements to your code in any arbitrary order.

```
import java.util.*;
import org.apache.commons.lang3.StringUtils;
import com.google.gson.stream.JsonReader;
import com.google.gson.Gson;
import java.io.*;
import java.awt.Event;
// etc.
```

---

[3]Specifically, a collection of selectable text items.

Thumbs Down!

Organizing imports mainly concerns readability. Style guides[4] recommend it because tidy and consistent import statements are more readable, and readability is a key factor in keeping code bug-free.

Typical guidelines you'll encounter include:

- Order imports alphabetically.

- In the case of hierarchical modules, group imports by top-level name. For example, all com.* imports come first, then net.*, then org.*, etc.

- Separate groups of similarly named modules with an empty line.

- If applicable, import using the full, absolute path. Don't use relative paths.[5]

- Consider renaming modules with very long names.[6]

A better-organized example of import statements would look something like this:

```
import java.awt.Event;
import java.io.File;
import java.util.ArrayList;
import java.util.HashSet;

import com.google.gson.Gson;
import com.google.gson.stream.JsonReader;

import org.apache.commons.lang3.StringUtils;
```

---

[4]For examples, see Google, 2017; Mozilla, 2017; Python, 2013.

[5]This rule doesn't apply in Java, which requires imports always to include the fully qualified package name.

[6]Again, this isn't possible in Java, but a language like Python, for example, allows you to write import statements like this: import really_longnamed_module as rlm.

Prevent Reuse

Every program has (at least) two purposes: the one for which it was written,
and another for which it wasn't.

—Alan Perlis (1982)

The software world raves about reuse. I'm sure you've already been implored by colleagues and teachers to write modular code that can easily be reused by others. But why should you allow freeloaders to make use of the code you bust your buns to write? If your colleagues want code, let them write it for themselves.

This section describes how you can clamp down on freeloading and prevent reuse on your project.

Shopping-List Subroutines

Let's start by looking at real-world examples of reusable modules to see what lessons we can learn—so we can avoid them.

Among the classes that a Java programmer typically uses early on when learning is a collection like the `ArrayList`, a class that was designed to be very reusable.[7]

For example, consider some of the methods that the `ArrayList` class provides:

- `add`: Appends the specified element to the end of a list

- `clear`: Removes all of the elements from a list

- `isEmpty`: Returns true if a list contains no elements

- `size`: Returns the number of elements in a list

- `subList`: Returns a view of the portion of this list between the specified `fromIndex`, inclusive, and `toIndex`, exclusive

- `toArray`: Returns an array containing all of the elements in this list in proper sequence (from first to last element)

---

[7]Keep in mind that the concept of a class includes some properties missing from the more general idea of a module (e.g., instantiation). However, we can still use things like classes and subroutines to demonstrate modular programming practices.

Each method performs one specific task. If you want an `ArrayList` object to carry out several tasks, you have to write a series of calls to several different methods.

However, as one anti-rule of programming tells us, *"Write modules with multiple purposes. Don't let them focus on only one task."* Imagine how much harder it would be to use the `ArrayList` if each method carried out not one but several tasks. For example:

- Instead of separate `add` and `size` methods, it had an `addAndReturnSize` method. This would mean you could only obtain the list's current size by first adding an item to it.

- Instead of separate `subList` and `toArray` methods, it had only a `subListToArray` method, meaning a sub-list could only be obtained in the form of an array and not a list.

Smooshing together several tasks into one subroutine can make it very hard to reuse. Doing them together might make sense for your particular use case, but it's unlikely to be useful to others. The less related those tasks are, the worse the problem gets.

```java
public void doVariousUnrelatedStuff() {
    System.out.println(supplier.getName());
    int price = product.getPrice() -
            product.getReduction();
    updatePrice(product, price);
    if (date.getMonth() == "December") {
        sendChristmasLeaflet(customer);
    }
}
```

A subroutine like this, which throws together random tasks like a shopping list, has little hope of being reused.

Thumbs Down!

Shopping-list subroutines can come about when an author focuses too much on their specific problem, thus combining several tasks in very specific ways. You create more reusable code by breaking a module's capabilities into individual, independent tasks and providing a subroutine for each one. Your colleagues will be grateful.

That doesn't mean you can't provide your own more-complex methods in addition. For example, you could start by writing a `Product` class (which represents something for sale) with two methods:

- `getPrice()`: Returns the price of this product

- `getReduction()`: Returns the amount by which this product is currently reduced (returns 0 if the product is not currently on offer)

Nevertheless, you could also provide a `getDiscountedPrice` method, which uses your `getPrice` and `getReduction` methods together to calculate the discounted price of the product.

```
return getPrice() - getReduction();
```

Ironically, hard-to-reuse methods can also come about when the author tries to guess in what manner a module will be reused and writes subroutines that attempt to do too much for the user. Trust your colleagues to combine those operations in whatever way they need for their purposes.

Just so you know, the degree to which a module remains focused on a single task is called cohesion and can be divided into several levels (Yourdon and Constantine, 1978). Levels of cohesion in descending order of acceptability include:

- Functional: The module performs a single task.

- Sequential: Several different tasks are grouped together because the output of one becomes the input of the next. For example, looking up a person's yearly income and then calculating which tax bracket they fall into.

- Communicational: Several different tasks are grouped into one module because they make use of the same data but are otherwise unrelated.

- Temporal: Several different tasks are grouped together because they're performed at the same time.

- Procedural: Several unrelated tasks are grouped together because they must be done in a specific order. For example, prompting the user to login before opening a sensitive file.

- Logical: Several tasks are grouped together; they're essentially unrelated, although they do logically similar things. For example, grouping together all the printing-related subroutines.

- Coincidental: The module groups together completely unrelated parts.

You should aim to write modules that are as cohesive as possible.

Mono-focused Modules

To curb reuse, you should really cut down a module's flexibility. A flexible module can work with different types, so try to ensure that yours focuses on as narrow a range of types as possible.

When working with primitive data types (i.e., built-in types like integers, floating-point numbers, characters, etc.) choose only the most restrictive ones. For example, when writing a subroutine that calculates the sum of an array of numbers, provide only an integer version:

```
int sum(int[] nums) {
    // ...
```

That leaves people trying to sum real numbers in the lurch, since real numbers can't be represented by an int. Attempting to pass real values to sum would cause a compile error.[8]

It's a similar story with custom types. For example, let's say it's your job to write a module that handles the registration of vehicles with a vehicle-licensing agency. The types in the system are already defined and modeled in Figure 8-1. The Vehicle type is a superclass to the Car, Motorcycle, and Truck types.

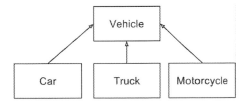

Figure 8-1. *Class diagram of the vehicle-registration program*

---

[8]This applies to statically typed languages like Java, where an object's type is declared.

All vehicles have a registration number, so your first attempt at a registration subroutine might look like this:

```
void register(Vehicle vehicle) {
    registrations.add(
            vehicle.getRegistrationNumber());
}
```

However, this misses an opportunity. A subroutine like this gives the module a flexible interface because the Vehicle type is a parent to numerous child types (like Car, Motorcycle, Truck, etc.). This means it will work with a variety of subtypes. One anti-rule nicely sums up what you're doing wrong (or rather, what you're inadvertently doing right): "*Root yourself in specific, concrete details. Always stop yourself if you begin to think in general terms, lest your code become generic and reusable.*"

Just like reducing the scope of the sum method, you could restrict the focus of the register method by allowing only a specific subtype as a parameter. Everything else can remain as before:

```
public void register(Car vehicle) {
    registrations.add(
            vehicle.getRegistrationNumber());
}
```

Now, for no good reason other than it frustrates your colleagues, the register method will only accept Car objects. Trying to pass other types like Truck or Motorcycle will cause a compile error. To register other types of vehicles in the future, additional work will need to be done.

Thumbs Down!

By allowing a module to work with a wider variety of types, you make it more reusable. Exactly how to do this depends on the language you use.

A statically typed language, like Java, requires you to declare a parameter's type. Thus, passing an object of the wrong type is caught at compile time. For primitive types, you could—if your language allows it—overload a subroutine by providing several versions, each with the same name but accepting differently typed parameters:

```
public double sum(double[] nums) { ... }

public int sum(int[] nums) { ... }

// etc.
```

For your own custom types, you could apply polymorphism, as the vehicle-registration example did. Chapter 9 will discuss polymorphism in more detail.

In a dynamically typed language,[9] where you aren't required to declare a variable's type, you should make sure the object is accessed only via the interface of the more generic type. For example, a `register` method in a dynamically typed language should only access the `vehicle` parameter via the interface of the `Vehicle` type. It shouldn't use methods or fields belonging exclusively to a subclass like `Car`.

Create Strong Dependencies

Programmers are most effective if shielded from, not exposed to, the innards of modules not their own. I dismissed [this] concept as a "recipe for disaster" . . . I was wrong.

—Fred Brooks (1995), discussing his reaction to information hiding

Modules in a program form connections with each other to get work done. For example, they might communicate via calls to and from one another, or via shared access to a common data set.

If you're new to programming, you might assume that the more a module knows about its collaborators the better. Even some of the most accomplished practitioners in software engineering, like Fred Brooks, originally thought this. They subsequently changed their minds after seeing the terrible trouble such an approach caused and recognizing that the reverse was true: things work better when modules don't expose their innards.

So, what happens if you purposefully avoid this revelation yourself and march on with that original assumption? This section explains.

---

[9]E.g., Python or Ruby.

Exposing Your Innards

Strong is better than weak, right? Any programmer would surely prefer the term *strong* be applied to an aspect of their program design. Similarly, tight is better than loose. Nobody wants to be told they have a loose screw.

Applying this logic to program design leads one to conclude that modules are better when they share strong, tight connections. Well, if that's what you want, there's no better way to achieve it than to have modules expose their internals to each other.

The simplest means of exposing a module's internals is to allow other modules to access its local data. How you do that depends on the language you use. In Java, where access to class members can be controlled, you can reveal a class's fields to the wider world by assigning them the access modifier public. This allows other classes to read and update those public fields.

For an example, let's go to the supermarket:

```java
public class Shop {
    // Keeps track of next available ID
    public static int nextID = 1;
}

public class BakeryProduct {
    // Uniquely identifies this type of product
    public int id;
    public BakeryProduct() {
        id = Shop.nextID++; }
    }
}

public class DairyProduct {
    public int id;
    public DairyProduct() {
        id = Shop.nextID++;
    }
}

// Plus lots more types of products...
```

When a new product is added to the Shop's line-up, the rule for creating a new identifier for the product is simple: take the next available ID number by looking up the nextID field in the Shop (and don't forget to increment the count in the process!). It looks simple, but the Shop class is very tightly connected to each of the different Product classes.

This doesn't create immediate problems. The fun comes later because tight connections between modules make the program wonderfully resistant to change.

For example, if the referenced field were to have its type altered, this would cause a problem. All uses of the field would have to be updated (in this example, changing nextID from long to int would mean the type of the id fields in each product would need altering accordingly). This is a more obvious problem because it would result in a compile-time error.

However, tight connections can be much more insidious. If they cause *runtime* errors, the compiler won't find them, and they might go undiscovered until after the program is released. For example, let's say your colleague updates the program after you and has to alter the way IDs are managed. Specifically, instead of assigning a product one ID, each product gets allocated a block of 100 consecutive IDs, the latter 99 of which get reserved for any later variants of that product.

That would mean, let's say, the BakeryProduct would need changing like this:

```
public class Shop {
    public static int nextID = 1;
}

public class BakeryProduct {
    public int id;
    public BakeryProduct() {
        id = Shop.nextID;
        Shop.nextID += 100;
    }
}
```

Because you made the connection tight, you forced your colleague to have to keep their wits about them. They mustn't neglect to update the rules that increase the ID number in *all* other product classes. If they fail to update all products in exactly the same way, they will cause a mess:

- If they forget to update even a single product class, that forgotten class will end up creating products that don't obey the rule. No space will be reserved for that product's variants in the ID range.

- If the ordering of the two statements is reversed in at least one class (i.e., 100 is added to `Shop.nextID` *before* assigning the value to `id`), the program will create empty holes and overlaps in the range of ID values.

Thumbs Down!

Modules have to communicate somehow if they're going to work together, but connections between modules aren't just a binary matter of being connected or not. These connections possess a strength that can vary, which is referred to as *coupling* (Yourdon and Constantine, 1978).

It's important to know this because inter-module couplings vary in strength. Put simply:

- A loose (or weak) coupling between modules means that changes in one module have little effect on the other. Loosely coupled modules are interchangeable, reusable, and easily testable.

- Tight (or strong) coupling between modules means that changes in one module easily create ripple effects that have repercussions on the other. Tightly coupled modules are hard to replace, difficult to reuse, a nightmare to test, and prone to error (Basili et al., 1996; Briand and Wüst, 2002). Your colleagues don't like tight coupling.

You can find out more about the different levels of coupling in any good source on software design. What follows is a brief summary.

At the looser/weaker end of coupling, you see levels like *message coupling* and *data coupling*. Message coupling happens when objects pass messages to each other. Each object encapsulates its own state and doesn't allow other objects to access it. Similarly, data coupling happens when modules share pieces of data with each other; for example, by passing parameters in a function call. These levels of coupling are considered routine and acceptable.

In the middle of the range, you come across *control coupling*, which happens when one module passes data to another module with the intent of controlling its behavior. For example, the following subroutine, lookupStudentsByNumber, accepts a "what-to-do" flag (lookupGraduates) that tells it whether or not it should include students who already graduated in the search.

```
/**
 * Build a list of Student profiles by looking
 * them up in the database by ID.
 *
 * @param studentIds
 *    The list of ids
 * @param lookupGraduates
 *    Whether to lookup graduated students (who are
 *    stored in a different database) or not.
 * @return The list of students found
 */
public List<Students> lookupStudentsByNumber(
        List<StudentId> studentIds,
        boolean lookupGraduates) {
    // ...
```

This sort of coupling requires that the calling module knows at least some things about how the other module functions. Control coupling is normally considered acceptable, although typically with caveats such as:

- Documentation should make the nature of control clear.

- The controlling parameter should be a "what's-going-on'" flag.[10]

At the tighter/stronger end of coupling, you find levels like *common coupling* or *content coupling*. Common coupling (where modules communicate indirectly by sharing the same data) will be seen later in this section.

An example of content coupling (where one module relies on the internal details of another) was seen earlier between the Shop class and the various Product classes. Such strong coupling is generally disapproved of, which is why many object-oriented

---

[10]Such a flag describes the current situation rather than instruct the module what to do. This allows the called module to make its own decisions in response.

languages (Java included) allow you to mark fields as `private`, thus hiding the information from other modules. The usual advice is to mark every field as private, until a *very* good reason arises that forces you to relax that restriction.

The Public Face of a Module

Rather than making a module expose its innards, your colleagues prefer you to write modules where internal information stays hidden. As usual with your colleagues' demands, that means more work for you.

If modules aren't permitted to communicate by fiddling with each other's internals, then each module has to have some means of receiving messages from others. This means you have to construct an interface for each module. In this case, the term *interface* refers to the public face a module presents to the world, the boundary past which only specific forms of information may travel.

After reading the previous section on strong coupling, you should now appreciate that loosely coupled interfaces are generally preferred. That means all information not explicitly accessible via an interface remains hidden. Unlike you, your colleagues derive comfort from knowing those hidden details can be altered without causing adverse ripple effects.

If you find your interface design is being carefully scrutinized to ensure coupling remains loose, you might wonder whether you have any options left open to you for causing trouble in this area.

Actually, there are a couple of remaining cards you might play.

First, you can work within the rules, but at the same time abuse them and take them to extremes. For example, passing information via parameter lists in a subroutine call (identified earlier as data coupling) is considered acceptable. However, applying the anti-rule *"In general, the bigger the better"* means you should create modules with lots of subroutines, each one accepting a huge list of parameters. Extreme size tends to tighten even acceptable types of coupling, because a module with many subroutines or a subroutine with a lot of parameters takes more work to connect it up with other modules.

Another option is to sneakily "go around" the interface without being caught. One particularly sly way is to create a form of common coupling. In this case, modules A and B don't actually share a direct link (as they would in the case of, say, a subroutine call from A to B). Instead, A and B both share access to the same object, C. This means A can affect the behavior of B (or vice versa) by changing the value of C.

To demonstrate this, let's go to the moon. The following code is taken from a program that controls a rocket, whose mission is to travel to the moon, dig up some rocks, and return them to Earth. Data shared among various modules in the program is stored in the DataStore object[11]:

```java
public class DataStore {
    private static DataStore store = null;

    // Current weight of the ship
    private double weight;

    private DataStore() { }

    public static DataStore getShipData() {
        if (store == null) {
            store = new DataStore();
        }
        return store;
    }

    public double getWeight() { return weight; }

    public void setWeight(double weight) {
        this.weight = wcight;
    }
}
```

Two classes involved in launching the rocket are the TrajectoryMapper and the FuelCalculator, each of which are written by different programming teams. Both depend on the rocket's current weight, which is obtained by a WeighingMachine. The TrajectoryMapper computes a trajectory for the rocket as follows:

```java
public class TrajectoryMapper {
    public void calculateTrajectory() {
        DataStore store = DataStore.getShipData();
        double weight;
```

---

[11]The DataStore is an example of a singleton (Gamma et al., 1995). It's designed in such a way that only one instance of a DataStore can be created. This same object is shared between every class that accesses the DataStore, creating a kind of global variable.

```
        if (store.getWeight() == 0.0) {
            weight = WeighingMachine.getWeight();
            store.setWeight(weight);
        }
        // Code for computing trajectory
        // based on weight here...
    }
}
```

While the FuelCalculator computes fuel-consumption rates necessary to get the rocket into space:

```
public class FuelCalculator {
    public void calculateFuelConsumption() {
        DataStore store = DataStore.getShipData();
        double weight;

        if (store.getWeight() == 0.0) {
            weight = WeighingMachine.getWeight();
            store.setWeight(weight);
        }
        // Code for calculating rocket
        // fuel consumptions here...
    }
}
```

Both classes first check whether the data store actually contains a weight measurement yet. If not, the weight is zero, and so the object gets the current weight and stores it in the DataStore.

All seems straightforward, right? However, the beautiful subtleties of indirect coupling can be deceiving.

First, the DataStore is essentially a global variable (or global object). This means you gain access to all the potential problems with global variables (discussed back in Chapter 3).

Second, the indirect, tight coupling makes the program sensitive to unintended side effects when updating the code. For example, imagine that the weighing machine is changed from one that reports weight in pounds to one that reports in kilograms. Since all teams were measuring in pounds beforehand, the `TrajectoryMapper` team update their code to convert this value into pounds before storing it, like this (changes to the code are underlined):

```
if (store.getWeight() == 0) {
    weight = WeighingMachine.getWeight();
    // Convert kilograms to pounds by multiplying
    // by 2.2
    store.setWeight(weight * 2.2);
}
```

The team writing the `FuelCalculator` also learns of the new weighing machine. However, they mistakenly assume that the `DataStore` now stores that weight in kilograms also. But since their class uses pounds, they decide to convert the value to pounds after looking it up in the `DataStore`. Hence, they make this change to their code:

```
if (store.getWeight() == 0.0) {
    weight = WeighingMachine.getWeight();
    store.setWeight(weight);
}
weight = weight * 2.2;
```

The result is that the weight used by the `FuelCalculator` is 4.4 times larger than the actual value. The rocket will therefore use too much fuel during the launch and go careering off into outer space never to be seen again.[12]

---

[12]You might think this scenario a bit far-fetched; rocket engineers making such an elementary mistake as to incorrectly convert between Imperial and SI units? But it's actually inspired by the true story of the Mars Climate Orbiter, lost in 1999 for very similar reasons.

Thumbs Down!

There's lots to say about writing good interfaces—too much for the space available here. However, just to get you started, a few basic expectations of interfaces you'll likely encounter include:

- Smaller is generally better:

  - A module should have a reasonable number of subroutines. As it grows, it becomes unwieldy and more error-prone (Tang, 1999). At this point, the module probably needs splitting to represent several finer-grained concepts.

  - Each subroutine should have a small number of parameters.[13]

- Each module should perform a single, well-defined task and cause minimal side effects (ideally none).

- What goes on inside a module should be kept hidden from outsiders so they're protected from any internal changes. This is especially true for volatile parts of a module.

  - In the case of object-oriented programming languages, this means giving class members the "strictest workable level of privacy" (Bloch, 2008).

- When modules communicate, prefer explicit, loosely coupled means like message-passing or subroutine calls (using parameters to pass information).

- Interfaces should be carefully documented. This includes descriptions of what task a module performs, what data it accepts and returns, and any information that counters the user's normal expectations (e.g., potential exceptions or side effects when calling a subroutine).

---

[13]See Chapter 6 (section "Abuse Parameters") for a discussion of this.

..

CHAPTER 9

Classes and Objects

Objectives

In this chapter, you'll learn:

- Some bad reasons to create classes

- How to make classes rigid and inflexible

- Lesser alternatives to polymorphism

- How to abuse inheritance in order to compromise your software design

Prerequisites

Before reading this chapter, make sure you're familiar with:

- The basic ideas behind object-oriented programming, particularly:

  - Instantiation and the difference between a class and an object

  - Composition (i.e., one class containing a reference to another class)

  - Inheritance

- Static methods

- Interfaces in Java, and the `interface` keyword

© Karl Beecher 2018
K. Beecher, *Bad Programming Practices 101*, https://doi.org/10.1007/978-1-4842-3411-2_9

Introduction

Like modular programming, object-oriented programming (OOP) attempts to mitigate the problems of building software at large scale. While the two approaches share common motivations and concerns—to the extent that much advice from modular programming is applicable to OOP—the OOP paradigm nevertheless does things quite differently. The chief difference is that the OOP approach yields programs made up of multiple interacting objects. Each object is constructed from a blueprint (a class) and is responsible for managing its own state and operations.

Object-oriented programming came to dominate software development in the 1990s. Its significance continues to this day, with the majority of contemporary, popular languages supporting the OOP paradigm. Like a latter-day digital Trojan horse, it has infiltrated projects far and wide. That means the nefarious lessons and nasty tricks this chapter discusses are widely applicable in today's software landscape.

Have Questionable Motives for Creating Classes

A class should represent a well-defined abstraction, not just a bundle of methods and variable definitions.

—Johnson and Foote, 1988

Before you even begin creating a new class, you'll be faced with certain questions that require careful answering: why am I creating this new class? What purpose does it serve? What concept from my problem does it represent? And how can I ignore these questions and do it all haphazardly instead?

The creation of a new class is a tricky thing because it's a design issue. Few hard rules govern exactly how and when a class should come into existence. That means the practices described in this section aren't bad in every situation. In fact, they might occasionally be considered acceptable.

But don't lose heart. If you follow the advice in this section repeatedly and without thought, you're bound to cause some pain eventually.

Data Classes

When working in an object-oriented environment, the dreaded word *responsibility* crops up a lot. Naturally, it sends shivers down your spine, but facing responsibility is kind of unavoidable in OOP.

146

Or is it?

OOP tries to make you design objects that are independent and responsible for looking after themselves and making their own decisions. Not only can this be tricky to do, but it would require you to break some of the key anti-rules of bad programming. Ask yourself: how can you follow the anti-rule *Prefer monolithic over modular code*" when responsibility (and therefore your code) has to be distributed around multiple classes?

Happily, a way exists for you to design classes that are powerless and devoid of responsibility. You can create a data class.

A data class is nothing more than a holder of data, a glorified record.[1] Here's an example of a book modeled as a data class:

```java
public class Book {
    private String author;
    private int numPages;
    private String isbn;

    public String getAuthor() { return author; }

    public void setAuthor(String author) {
        this.author = author;
    }

    public int getNumPages() { return numPages; }

    public void setNumPages(int numPages) {
        this.numPages = numPages;
    }

    public String getIsbn() { return isbn; }

    public void setIsbn(String isbn) {
        this.isbn = isbn;
    }
}
```

As you can see, a data class typically has little more than a collection of fields and corresponding accessor methods. You can do little else with this Book than get and set its properties.

---

[1]A record is a simple data structure that groups together a collection of fields.

Designing your classes as data classes is great because it saves you the effort of having to do any proper design work.

Thumbs Down!

When a data class appears, that raises the question, "Where is the code responsible for manipulating its values?" That code must lie elsewhere.

For example, when using the Book class, the program needs to check certain values, like ensuring numPages is not negative or validating the format of the ISBN. The natural place for such code would probably be inside the Book class. Putting it outside the class raises the likelihood that the same code is duplicated in several locations because those checks are required in different places in the program.

As Martin Fowler writes, "Data classes are like children. They are okay as a starting point, but to participate as a grownup object, they need to take some responsibility" (Fowler, 1999).

For more on this, see the section "Make Objects Inflexible."

God Classes

It's all well and good to follow the preceding advice and create mostly data classes, but at some point you have to consider where the bulk of your program's logic will actually reside. It has to go somewhere, right?

Be mindful of a couple of anti-rules, particularly *"In general, the bigger the better"* and, again, *"Prefer monolithic code over modular code."* You can save yourself a lot of design effort by simply stuffing the bulk of your logic into a tiny number of "mega"-classes. Let those objects orchestrate everything. Put them at the center of the program, ordering around all the other powerless objects.

Because this concentrates enormous power into their hands, such classes are usually termed *god classes*. How can anyone argue against something with such an awesome name?

Thumbs Down!

God classes are actually quite easy to argue against, and your colleagues will probably do so. In many cases, they'll simply be referencing the same objections from earlier chapters.

Consider the consequences on coupling and cohesion. The same principles—prefer loose coupling and high cohesion—also apply to OOP:

- An object that exerts heavy control on the behavior of so many others tightens coupling.

- An object that manipulates a diverse array of objects possesses many unrelated responsibilities, thus lowering its cohesion. The consequences of both are discussed at length in Chapter 8.

God classes tend to create maintenance and testing headaches. Your colleagues prefer a class to represent a single, distinct abstraction that focuses on one aspect of the problem.

Utility Classes

Another way you can dodge this object-oriented design malarkey is to bend your object-oriented language into producing old-fashioned procedural code. In Java, you can do this by designing classes as a set of static methods.

```java
public class BookUtils {

    public static boolean validateIsbn(Book b) { }

    public static boolean validateNumPages(Book b) { }

    public static void regsiterBookInLibraryOfCongress(
            Book b) { }

    // etc...
}
```

By doing this, your new class becomes little more than a library of routines. No need to worry about OOP principles and design. What a weight off your mind!

Thumbs Down!

Personally, I wouldn't say utility classes are inherently bad (plenty of perfectly good projects have a utility class here and there). You should simply be aware that using them means giving up certain features of object orientation. Your colleagues may be unwilling to tolerate this in all cases, especially when a superior object-oriented solution exists.

For example, a utility class can neither be instantiated nor extended by being sub-typed (Bloch, 2008). However, a key OOP principle states that new behavior should be added to a class by extending it rather than modifying it.[2] Since sub-typing a utility class is off the table, you can't adhere to this principle in this case, because you can't extend a utility class.

Make Objects Inflexible

OOP is often sold on its ability to produce flexible designs. Do things right and you can produce classes that are more easily maintained and reused. Do things not-so-right and the resulting inflexibility can cause programming nightmares.

Objects Obeying Orders

OOP design claims objects should be independent and able to make their own decisions. On the surface, this sounds great. A load of work off your hands, right?

But don't forget that the job of making them independent falls to you. Instilling independence and responsibility into objects is like imbuing your kids with the same characteristics. It takes patience, hard work, and careful thought. Paradoxically, then, you can give yourself an easier time (in the short term, at least) by being tyrannical with your objects.

To put it another way, it's easier to make your objects cross the road on command than to teach them how to do it by themselves.

But decisions have to be made somewhere. Instead of dividing up decision-making power between the objects in your program, you'll have to concentrate that power in a tiny handful of quasi-omnipotent objects who order all the others around. As a consequence, most objects in your project will end up being treated like children.

To establish this domineering relationship, a decision-making class is composed of references to numerous powerless classes. Then, all decisions that ought to be made by a "child" should be encoded into the "parent" instead.

---

[2]Known as the Open/Closed principle, meaning the class should be open for extension but closed for modification.

The following example depicts a tyrannical parent (StationManager, which aspires to tightly control all aspects of running a train station) and one of its children (TicketMachine, a ticket-vending machine).

```java
class StationManager {
    // StationManager is composed of lots of other classes
    // (like HelpDesk, StationDisplay, SpeakerSystem
    // etc.) in addition to the TicketMachine
    TicketMachine machine = new TicketMachine();

    public void insertCoinToMachine(int coinValue) {
        machine.setCredit(coinValue);
    }

    public void buyTicket() {
        Ticket t = chooseTicket();
        if (t.getPrice() <= machine.getCredit()) {
            machine.deduct(t.getPrice());
            printTicket();
        }
        else {
            System.out.println("Not enough credit!");
        }
    }
}

class TicketMachine {
    int credit;

    public int getCredit() { return credit; }

    public void setCredit(int value) { credit = value; }

    public void deduct(int value) { credit -= value; }
}
```

The TicketMachine has been taught how to do almost nothing. The StationManager keeps it on a very short leash, allowing it to do barely anything on its own initiative. The TicketMachine lives its life following orders from the StationManager. This makes designing the TicketMachine very simple for you.

Thumbs Down!

You might recognize that the two classes in the previous example, `StationManager` and `TicketMachine`, are instances of a god class and a data class respectively.[3] This should immediately ring alarm bells.

It should also indicate where the design is lacking. OOP design recommends that objects manage the concepts they were designed to represent. When deciding where to put the code for a particular task, you should ask questions like, "Which object is responsible for this?" or "Whose business should this be?"

In this case, the responsibility for processing a ticket sale belongs to the `TicketMachine`. It's really no business of any other class.

```
class TicketMachine {
    private int credit;

    public void insertCoin(int value) {
        credit += value;
    }

    public void buyTicket() {
        Ticket t = chooseTicket();
        if (t.getPrice() <= credit) {
            credit -= t.getPrice();
            printTicket();
        }
        else {
            displayMessage("Not enough credit!");
        }
    }
}
```

Giving a `TicketMachine` responsibility for its own business yields several benefits:

- It puts relevant functionality in its logical place, thus making it easier to find.

---

[3]See the earlier section, "Have Questionable Motives for Creating Classes."

- It reduces the number of responsibilities of the controlling class (in this case, `StationManager`). Like subroutines and modules, classes ought to have a single responsibility.[4]

- Removing responsibilities from it reduces the size of the controlling class, which is a good thing given that large classes tend to be more error-prone (Basili et al., 1996; Gyimóthy et al., 2005).

- It enables classes like `TicketMachine` to do a better job of hiding their implementation details behind an interface.

  - Note that the newer version of `TicketMachine` no longer provides methods in concrete terms of getting/setting internal fields (such as `credit`); rather, its methods deal with more conceptual terms, i.e., inserting coins and buying tickets.

Rigid Relationships

An object-oriented programming course tells you many things, particularly about design. It tells you objects collaborate in solving a problem, that they work together by establishing relationships and passing messages to each other. You'll be told objects should be able to choose which other objects to collaborate with.

You, however, with your trust issues, prefer behaving like a tyrannical parent. No way will your "children" be allowed to make decisions like that out of your sight. Decisions concerning whom they can be "friends" with remain yours.

Doing this requires you to be the enforcer of strong, rigid relationships between classes and is another great way to bake inflexibility into your program design. Check out this snippet from a program that manages the feeding of pets:

```
class PetFeeder {
    public void giveFood(Dog d) {
        d.feed();
    }
}
```

---

[4]This is called the Single Responsibility Principle (Martin, 2009).

```
class Dog {
    public void feed() {
        System.out.println("Wolfing down dog food");
    }
}

public static void main(String[] args) {
    PetFeeder feeder = new PetFeeder();
    Dog lassie = new Dog();
    feeder.giveFood(lassie);
}
```

Seems simple enough, but little would you suspect that this straightforward design has a strong element of rigidity.

To expose it, let's imagine your colleague subsequently comes along and, for some inexplicable reason, has a pet cat. They wish to add their pet type to the system:

```
class Cat {
    public void feed() {
        System.out.println("Turning nose up at cat food");
    }
}
```

They also want the program feed their cat:

```
public static void main(String[] args) {
    PetFeeder feeder = new PetFeeder();
    Dog lassie = new Dog();
    feeder.giveFood(lassie);

    Cat felix = new Cat();
    feeder.giveFood(felix);
}
```

Of course, the laws of evolution conspire to prevent this from working:

```
error: incompatible types:Cat cannot be converted to Dog
    feeder.giveFood(felix);
                    ^
```

That's because you originally gave the PetFeeder the ability to feed only dogs. To feed a cat, the PetFeeder requires an extra method be added to it:

```
class PetFeeder {
    public void giveFood(Dog d) {
        d.feed();
    }

    public void giveFood(Cat c) {
        c.feed();
    }
}
```

So, if your friend wants to feed their moggy, you force them to do extra work. That serves them right for liking cats in the first place.

Thumbs Down!

The problem doesn't just lie with cats. Adding any new type of pet to the system, be it a rabbit, a spider, or a lizard, requires the addition of new giveFood methods.

This means the PetFeeder has the potential to grow into a very large class full of giveFood methods. Although each feed method would technically be doing something different, the *concept* of giving food to a pet is the same in each case. In other words, the same message is sent to each type of pet. This makes it a form of duplication, and don't forget that unnecessary duplication in software gets right up your colleagues' noses.

The problem stems from the original decision to make the PetFeeder deal with concrete classes[5] like Dog. This is known as *programming to an implementation*. A key design principle in OOP states you should instead prefer *programming to an interface*. This means that classes should, where possible, make references to more abstract classes.

What would be a more abstract class in our example? Pet dogs, pet cats, pet mice . . . they're all pets, and every pet needs feeding.

```
interface Pet {
    void feed();
}
```

---

[5]A concrete class is a class with no missing implementation details, unlike, say, an abstract class or interface.

Every pet gets fed, but each in a different way, so that detail is missing from the interface. Concrete implementations of Pet fill in that detail, for example:

```
class Mouse implements Pet {
    public void feed() {
        System.out.println("Nibbling on cheese.");
    }
}
```

What's the benefit of doing this? Well, for one thing, the duplication in PetFeeder can be eliminated.

```
class PetFeeder {
    public void giveFood(Pet p) {
        p.feed();
    }
}
```

The revised version of PetFeeder is programmed to an interface rather than an implementation. Instead of enforcing a rigid relationship between two concrete classes, the PetFeeder can now deal with any class that implements the Pet interface (because every Pet must have a feed method). Consequently, PetFeeder only needs a single giveFood method to feed all pets.

Avoid Polymorphism

No doubt all this talk of flexibility from the preceding section leaves you thoroughly unimpressed. Flexibility is all very well for contortionists, but you don't need it in your life. It just makes work harder for you.

That idea from the previous section—that of providing a single interface for communicating with numerous different types—actually has a name: *polymorphism*. The OOP community is quite fond of it, so it can be hard to avoid.

Short of avoiding it entirely, you could at least do it in undesirable ways. This section will demonstrate how.

A program sometimes has to make decisions based on which type it's currently dealing with, as with the previous example and its various types of pets who needed feeding in different ways. The second version featuring the Pet interface (the one no doubt preferred by your colleagues) was a polymorphic version. That's because the Pet type was an abstract interface that hid from the using type a variety of different concrete implementations.

Since polymorphism is so lauded, you might suspect you have to choose between doing it right or not doing it at all. However, you have another choice. You could use an approach that *appears* as though you're trying to build a flexible, polymorphic solution, but actually engenders a degree of rigidity in the program. Look at this example code from a supermarket checkout program, which gets the prices for a list of groceries.

```
ArrayList<Object> shoppingList = getShoppingList();

for (Object item : shoppingList) {
    int price = 0;
    if (item instanceof ScanItem) {
        // Scan the barcode and lookup the price
        price = item.lookupPrice();
    }
    else if (item instanceof ProduceItem) {
        // Produce is sold by weight
        price = item.getPriceByWeight();
    }
    else if (item instanceof ReducedItem) {
        // Reduced items require the human operator
        // to key in the price on the tag
        price = item.keyInPrice();
    }

    System.out.println(price)
}
```

A couple of design decisions make it inflexible, hopefully in ways that go unnoticed.

First, since groceries come in all different types, the containing list is declared as containing Object types (the one type in Java that all other types derive from). After all, you can't be sure exactly which types are in the list, but you can at least be sure that they're Objects. Beyond that incidental detail, however, an Object shares no conceptual relationship with the various grocery types, making it awkward to deal with the contents of the list.

Second, each type of grocery is priced in different ways, such as being scanned, weighed, or keyed in manually. That's why each type has different methods for obtaining the price. By testing each grocery's type, you make it appear to the observer like you're trying to take into account the problems of mixed types. However, that sneaks in some nice, subtle problems at the same time:

- The if ladder in this code can potentially grow very long as you add more types of groceries, and lengthy chains of if statements always provide good fun.

- The moment you introduce a new type of grocery and neglect to add an extra clause to the if ladder, the program ceases functioning correctly because it doesn't know how to handle the new type of grocery. With luck, the code contains multiple if ladders, just like this one testing groceries' types. The more ladders there are, the more likely that one or more of them go forgotten.

Thumbs Down!

Don't be surprised when extensive use of the instanceof keyword (or whatever equivalent your language has for checking type equality) raises eyebrows among your colleagues.

It would do so in this case because the checkout code, like the pet example before it, is programmed to a concrete implementation. The instanceof keyword is being used to see if an object is of a specific concrete type.

You'll find your code more readily acceptable if it is instead programmed to an abstract interface. But how can you do that when the program deals with a collection of differently typed objects?

First, you can apply the lesson from the previous section and create an interface for all those grocery types. The exact method for obtaining a price might vary, but that doesn't matter. We know one thing for sure: all groceries have a price.

```
interface Grocery {
    int getPrice();
}
```

Now, each concrete item can report a price via the same method. For example:

```
// A ProduceItem for example is a type of Grocery that
// gets a price by weighing the item.
public class ProduceItem implements Grocery
{
    // Cents per kilogram
    private int pricePerKg;

    public ProduceItem(int pricePerKg) {
        this.pricePerKg = pricePerKg;
    }

    public int getPrice() {
        // Ask the Scales class to weigh this item
        return Scales.getWeight(this) * pricePerKg;
    }
}
```

All these different types can go into the same shopping list thanks to the Liskov Substitution Principle (Martin, 1996). This states that an object of a particular type should be replaceable by any other object of the same type or its sub-type. That's why you might see code like this:

```
List<Integer> numbers = new ArrayList<Integer>();
```

The type on the left is abstract. The type on the right is a concrete class. You could, for example, pass this variable to a subroutine like this:

```
// Returns sum of the nums.
Integer sum(List<Integer> nums) { // ...
```

You could subsequently change the instantiation of numbers to be a LinkedList instead:

```
List<Integer> numbers = new LinkedList<Integer>();
```

But nothing else in the program would need to change, because a `LinkedList` is still a `List`.[6] Similarly, if you started with this:

```
Pet lassie = new Dog();
feeder.giveFood(lassie);
```

and you subsequently discovered you'd made a mistake and that Lassie was actually a cat (nobody's perfect), you could alter the code in just one place and the rest would still work:

```
Pet lassie = new Cat();
feeder.giveFood(lassie);
```

Because of this principle, you can treat all the diverse types in a collection in a uniform way:

```
List<Grocery> shoppingList = getShoppingList();

for (Grocery item : shoppingList) {
    int price = item.getPrice();
    System.out.println(price)
}
```

Now, everything in the list is a grocery. The loop doesn't care what specific type, only that each item will answer when it receives the message `getPrice()`. No matter how many additional types of groceries you add, this loop can remain unchanged and still total the price correctly.

Overuse and Abuse Inheritance

When all you have is a hammer, every problem looks like a nail.

—Proverb

Inheritance is among the earliest of the neat tricks learned in a typical OOP course. Like every neat trick you learn, inheritance should immediately become your figurative "hammer," the tool you have in hand now that every problem looks like a nail.

---

[6]Because both `ArrayList` and `LinkedList` implement the `List` interface.

Going Deep

Inheritance may well have been sold to you as a means of extending classes. You take an existing class and augment its features by inheriting from it and adding new members.

For example, let's say you begin with a Car class, and then later you want to model your new Land Rover. But that's not just any old car. It's a sexy four-wheel-drive car whose awesomeness cannot be captured adequately by such a vanilla type as Car. It deserves its own class. And so you extend the existing Car class and create a FourWheelDriveCar class. Figure 9-1 depicts this.

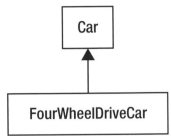

Figure 9-1. *One class inherits from another*

```
class Car {
    // ...
}

class FourWheelDriveCar extends Car {
    // Activate 4-wheel-drive mode
    public void activate4WD() {
        // ...
    }
}
```

Once you see this problem as a nail, there's no limit to how much you can use inheritance as a hammer. For every additional feature you want to introduce, you can simply extend the existing, less detailed class. Go crazy. Go deep.

Of course, this repeated extension results in a deep inheritance hierarchy (see Figure 9-2), but who cares?

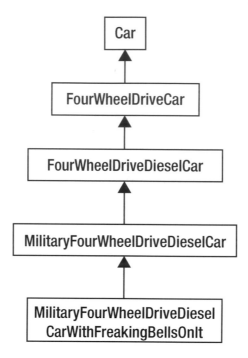

Figure 9-2. *A five-level-deep inheritance hierarchy*

Thumbs Down!

Actually, a deep inheritance hierarchy could well raise complaints. Going beyond a certain depth can cause serious problems for testing and maintenance.

In terms of comprehension, it makes the job harder for the reader. It can be difficult to see which methods or fields a deep class actually provides, because it has potentially inherited dozens or even hundreds of them via its many superclasses. In a famous study of OOP design practices (which examined real-world code examples), one inheritance hierarchy reached eight levels deep. The class at this level had only four methods of its own, but it supported 132 methods given to it by its ancestors (Chidamber and Kemerer, 1994).

Things get even harder to understand when you realize that some of those inherited methods have surely been overridden by one or more of the classes in the middle of the hierarchy. Determining which version of a method the deepest class provides then becomes frustratingly difficult.

A deep inheritance hierarchy also has great potential for causing ripple effects. Altering the behavior of a class at the higher levels can suddenly change that of its descendants in unintended ways. That's because inheriting from a concrete class creates a tight coupling between parent and children, and—as Chapter 8 told you—tight coupling encourages unintended knock-on effects. Doing this amidst a deep inheritance hierarchy only intensifies the problem because the ripple effects travel far.

Several studies suggest that the deeper a class sits in an inheritance hierarchy, the more error-prone and costly to maintain it is, especially when many methods are involved (see, for example, Basili et al., 1996; Briand and Wüst, 2002; Prechelt et al., 2003).

Judging to what maximum depth an inheritance tree should be allowed to go is still seemingly up for debate. You'll see figures ranging from around three or four levels (Microsoft, 2016) up to about ten (CA-CST-SII, 2015). In my own view, you should strongly prefer the lower of those two suggestions.

Quick and Dirty Reuse

If you want to reuse code (or, more likely, you're forced into reusing it) and that code lies in another class, why not use inheritance? It's easy. Your class can just inherit from the class containing the code to be reused, because inheritance automatically gives you access to all the methods in the parent.

To demonstrate, here's a little sample from a program that models animal behavior. The program already includes a Bird class, which someone else is responsible for:

```
class Bird {
    boolean flying = false;

    public void fly() {
        flying = true;
        System.out.println("I'm flying!");
    }
}
```

Your job is to add another class modeling bats. Your new Bat class needs a fly method, something the Bird class already contains. To make your job simpler, you can make Bat inherit from Bird to gain access to the fly method:

```
class Bat extends Bird {
    public void squeak() {
```

```
        System.out.println("'Squeak, squeak!'");
    }
}
```

That works, right? Let's see:

```
Bat batsy = new Bat();
batsy.squeak();
batsy.fly();
```

When you run the preceding code, everything works as expected:

```
'Squeak, squeak!'
I'm flying!
```

You added the required functionality, so, job done. But, like setting a trap, you've also sown the seeds of a problem.

The coder responsible for the Bird class adds another behavior to it: laying eggs. Their class now looks like this:

```
class Bird {
    boolean flying = false;
    int eggs;

    public void fly() {
        flying = true;
        System.out.println("I'm flying!");
    }

    public void layEggs(int n) {
        eggs += n;
        System.out.println("Laid " + eggs + " eggs");
    }
}
```

They've sprung the trap. Because your Bat class inherits everything in Bird, your program now models bats as being capable of laying eggs!

Thumbs Down!

Inheritance is one of the most commonly misused techniques in the OOP toolbox, and misusing it often results in an inflexible, hard-to-maintain codebase. Consequently, you should think carefully before deciding to use it.

Keep in mind that it creates a relationship between two classes, C and D, often called an *is-a* relationship. That's because when class D inherits from class C, you can say D *is a* C. In the previous example, Bat inherits Bird just to reuse some code. This abuses inheritance because that relationship doesn't make semantic sense—a bat is *not* a bird, and being able to fly doesn't make it one.

OOP specialists recommend against using inheritance just for code reuse. The consensus is that inheritance actually serves best as a means to capture variations among some abstract concepts. We saw this earlier when we defined Dog and Cat as more specific varieties of Pet, or ProduceItem and ScanItem as more specific varieties of Grocery. However, the previous example defined a Bat as a variety of Bird, and that makes no sense.

There's a more suitable use of inheritance in this example. In order to capture the variations, you have to first identify the abstract concepts. In this case, the program models animal behavior, so the abstract concepts are the traits or behaviors shared by many varieties of animal, like flying or egg laying. Just for starters, that would give us the following abstractions:

```
interface Flyer {
    void fly();
}

interface EggLayer {
    void layEggs(int n);
}
```

And so:

- Because a bat can fly, the Bat class is a variety of Flyer.

- Because a bird can fly and lay eggs, the Bird class is a variety of both Flyer and EggLayer.

```
class Bird implements Flyer, EggLayer {
    boolean flying = false;
    int eggs;
```

```java
    public void fly() {
        flying = true;
        System.out.println("I'm flying!");
    }

    public void layEggs(int n) {
        eggs += n;
        System.out.println("Laid " + eggs + " eggs");
    }
}

class Bat implements Flyer {
    boolean flying = false;

    public void fly() {
        flying = true;
        System.out.println("I'm flying!");
    }
}
```

This might improve the use of inheritance, but it forces us to implement the fly method multiple times. The original goal was to define the method once and reuse it. This is where your choice of language matters. For example, you could turn Flyer into some kind of partial class that contains an implementation of fly but isn't meant to be instantiated, only inherited. This corresponds to an abstract class in Java parlance. However, Java doesn't allow the multiple inheritance of classes as some languages do, so an animal class wouldn't be able to inherit multiple behaviors this way, as Bird should.

(If you use another language, you might be in a position to use techniques like mixins or traits. However, we'll remain focused on Java here.)

Since Java 8, a simple way to create a reusable fly method would be to use default methods.[7] This creates a single, default implementation of a method that all concrete classes inherit when they implement an interface.

---

[7]Ways also exist to do this without the use of inheritance; for example, by using certain design patterns. However, since this section focuses on inheritance, I'll stick with that.

```java
interface Flyer {
    void setFlying(boolean flying);

    default void fly() {
        setFlying(true);
        System.out.println("I'm flying!");
    }
}

class Bat implements Flyer {
    boolean flying = false;

    public void setFlying(boolean flying) {
        this.flying = flying;
    }
}

class Bird implements Flyer, EggLayer {
    boolean flying = false;

    public void setFlying(boolean flying) {
        this.flying = flying;
    }

    public void layEggs(int n) {
        eggs += n;
        System.out.println("Laid " + eggs + " eggs");
    }
}
```

This means the fly method is now available in both the Bird and Bat classes, it's defined in one place, and the inheritance hierarchy hasn't been compromised to achieve all that.

CHAPTER 10

Testing

Objectives

In this chapter, you'll learn:

- How to protect your code from tests that threaten to reveal bugs, in particular by

    - retaining authorship of tests;

    - doing the bare minimum necessary; and

    - writing untestable programs.

- How to write tests that cause havoc for your colleagues, in particular by

    - making a test's success dependent on its environment;

    - creating work for testers by unnecessarily widening the focus of a test; and

    - adding volatile, uncontrollable elements.

Prerequisites

Before reading this chapter, it will help if you're familiar with the following:

- The basic concepts of unit testing and integration testing

- How to write basic test cases using automated test frameworks like JUnit

© Karl Beecher 2018
K. Beecher, *Bad Programming Practices 101*, https://doi.org/10.1007/978-1-4842-3411-2_10

Introduction

Testing is a big part of the software-development process, so big that it's broken up into various stages, typically something like this:

- Unit testing: where individual pieces of the program are tested, typically at the level of routines in a module

- Integration testing: where several modules are tested together

- System testing: where the system as a whole is executed by the team to verify functionality

- Acceptance testing: where the system as a whole is executed by the customer to ensure it meets expectations

These stages grow progressively more important and involve more people as you go down the list. A low-level grunt like you has little hope of messing up testing during the latter stages, since they're often carried out collectively and under the watchful eyes of a responsible senior team member.

However, you can exert influence during the earlier two stages—unit and integration testing—where you have a chance of being left to your own devices. This chapter therefore focuses on the earlier testing stages, where you test the individual units[1] of code.

You know your own modules and subroutines well. You know where the bugs are hiding, and you want them to stay there. Consequently, you must carry out testing ineffectively so that the bugs are left well alone.

Be Protective of Your Code

You should do what you can to keep prying eyes away from your code. If you allow others to see it and test it, you risk all your lovely bugs being discovered. This section describes how you can protect your code.

---

[1]A unit is a small, testable part of a program, commonly at the level of an individual subroutine.

Keeping It to Yourself

It should go without saying that if you can avoid writing tests for your code, then for heaven's sake do so. However, the chances are good that you'll find yourself on a project whose leaders insist all program code be tested.

If this is the case, you should fight to be able write tests for your own code. Argue that, since you're the author of the code, you're most familiar with it and therefore in the best position to test it. If you allow your colleagues to test it instead, they won't take care with it, and anything that's as fragile as your code will break pretty quickly.

Thumbs Down!

That last sentence describes the whole point of appointing someone other than a unit's author to write tests for it.

As the proud author of a piece of code, you're too likely to go easy on your precious creation and *really* put it to the test. On the other hand, your colleague is positively salivating at the prospect of putting your code through the ringer. The opportunity to expose someone else's problems is just too rewarding to resist, so they'll naturally throw everything they can at your code to make it crumble. It's a good thing that they do, because seeing how well the code stands up to pummelling is the best way to demonstrate its quality.

In addition to their naked ambition, your colleague's lack of knowledge about the code is actually a benefit, not a drawback. You know how it's supposed to work, so you'll probably (unconsciously) test it in that specific way. However, your colleague is more likely to use the code in ways that are correct but unexpected; ways that you didn't anticipate and that might very well expose a bug.

Doing the Bare Minimum

If you succeed in getting your way and are able to test your own code, then you can go easy on it. You probably won't get away with writing zero tests, but writing a *bit* of test code that verifies little or nothing of the unit's behavior might just be enough to sneak past your team's prying eyes.

In other words, hope that your test is seen to be written, but not written to be seen.

If you want to be *really* brazen, write a test case like this:

```
public class MainTest {
    @Test
    public void testMyMethod() {
        assertTrue(true);
    }
}
```

A test that checks whether true is true will pass forever until the end of time. Of course, even someone giving your test a cursory glance will notice what you've done, so this approach is probably too risky.

Instead, you could test the absolute bare minimum. Remember that the point of unit testing is to build confidence in the absence of errors by demonstrating the unit withstands scrutiny from a comprehensive range of tests. So, a minimal range of tests (preferably a single one) won't elicit much confidence, but it might just fool others that you're testing earnestly.

For example, let's say you're testing a FizzBuzz routine.

```
String fizzBuzz(int n)
```

It calculates the correct response for a particular number, n, in a game of FizzBuzz. In this game, players take turns counting up from one. However:

- Numbers cleanly divisible by three must be replaced by the word "Fizz."

- Numbers cleanly divisible by five must be replaced by the word "Buzz".

- Numbers cleanly divisible by both those numbers must be replaced by the word "FizzBuzz."

- All other numbers remain unchanged (although `fizzBuzz` returns them as a string).

Since the `fizzBuzz` routine can respond in different ways under different conditions, it requires several tests (at least one for each different response) to build confidence in its stability.

However, you're not interested in building confidence in anything, so one test will suffice:

```
public class FizzBuzzTest {
    @Test
    public void testFizzBuzz() {
        FizzBuzzGame game = new FizzBuzzGame();
        String response = game.fizzBuzz(4);

        assertEquals(response, "4");
    }
}
```

Whatever you do, *don't* be tempted to build up a whole suite of test cases with lots of different input data. You'll only end up exposing problems in the program.

Thumbs Down!

Thoroughly testing a unit of code requires a good amount of forethought.

That's because exhaustive testing is rarely a realistic possibility. Even something as simple as square(n)—a subroutine that returns n multiplied by itself—would require many millions of executions for each possible value of n to show empirically that it works for all possible values. Something only slightly more complicated, like max(a, b), which returns the highest value from two numbers, a and b, would require a prohibitive number of tests thanks to combinatorial explosion.

Therefore, you have to be more methodical and design a relatively small set of tests that maximizes testing potential. One approach is a useful black-box technique[2] called equivalence partitioning. When applying this method, you examine the inputs to a unit and divide all possible values into groups based on the expected behavior they elicit. These groups are called equivalence classes. The inputs in each group elicit different outputs, but all values in a single group are assumed to elicit the same sort of behavior.

Instead of testing all values, we choose one value from each equivalence class to be a representative of all values of their class. It is assumed that only one value from each class is required to expose any potential errors.

---

[2]Black-box testing assumes you're unaware of the unit's inner workings. Applicable when you're not the unit's author or for designing test cases before a unit's implementation exists.

In the fizzBuzz subroutine example, the equivalence classes of the input, n, include the following:

- Normal acceptable numbers (e.g., 8): All acceptable numbers not divisible by 3 or 5. The method should return the same number we give it. If this number works, it implies all other numbers in this class also work.

- Fizzes (e.g., 3): All numbers divisible by three. Method should return "Fizz."

- Buzzes (e.g., 10): All numbers divisible by five. Method should return "Buzz."

- FizzBuzzes (e.g., 30): All numbers divisible by both three and five. Method should return "FizzBuzz."

And, because one piece of testing wisdom warns us that "bugs lurk in corners and congregate around boundaries" (Bezier, 1990):

- Acceptable boundary (e.g., 1): This should work.

- Unacceptable boundary (e.g., 0): This should be rejected.

Those equivalence classes are represented in Figure 10-1.

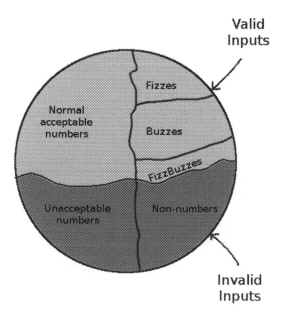

Figure 10-1. *Equivalence classes of inputs to FizzBuzz represented pictorially*

With just a bit of planning, we've come up with seven tests that cover all different situations. When all tests pass, it establishes a good level of confidence in the subroutine.

Many testing frameworks also make it easy to apply code-coverage reporting. This is a white-box technique[3] that shows which lines of code are executed during tests and which are not. The idea is that you can be more confident that executed lines don't contain bugs.

Code-coverage reports normally give results as the percentage of a unit's lines executed during a test. Generally, a unit subjected to high coverage probably has fewer bugs in it than a unit with low coverage. Let's use the FizzBuzz subroutine again as an example and imagine that the equivalence classes identified were turned into tests and executed. A coverage report might look like this:

```
public String fizzBuzz(int n) {
>     String output = "";
>     if (n < 1) {
>         return "Error: number must be positive";
>     }
>     if (n % 3 == 0) {
>         output += "Fizz";
>     }
>     if (n % 5 == 0) {
>         output += "Buzz";
>     }
>     return output.isEmpty() ? Integer.toString(n) : output;
}
```

Lines prefixed with a '>' symbol show which lines were executed during tests. As you can see, the equivalence classes identified cover lines of code inside the method.

---

[3]White-box testing assumes you're aware of the unit's inner workings.

Thwarting Efforts

You might find that policy prevents you from testing your own precious code. Thus, your callous colleagues will rip your baby from your arms and toss it uncaringly at someone else for examination.

In such circumstances, it might seem all is lost. The colleague testing your code is unlikely to go easy on it, as you would, so it's only a matter of time before your colleague roots out all the bugs. But actually, you can prepare for such outcomes before the testing phase. Specifically, you should try to make the code hard to test, dooming your colleagues' efforts to failure.

Earlier chapters in this book have already given you some tips that, among other things, make testing harder. Here's a summary of the important ones:

- Give the code poor layout. This makes white-box testing harder because poorly laid out code is difficult to understand.

- Don't document your code. This makes it hard to determine what each unit is supposed to do and come up with suitable tests for it.

- Use global variables. These are frustrating during tests because the tester cannot focus solely on the unit in question.

- Write highly complex units. Complex code has numerous possible pathways through it, meaning the tester has to write lots of test cases.

  - As a follow-on from this, include complex expressions in your conditions. Not only are they hard to understand, but compound expressions also increase the number of tests required.

- Prefer large, monolithic routines. Don't break them into small, focused subroutines. Large subroutines require more effort to understand before being tested.

- Give subroutines a large number of parameters. Such subroutines require more effort to test.

- Provide missing or poorly written error information. This makes it hard for a tester to reconstruct events from a failed test.

- Ensure your modules have lots of dependencies. When testing a module, its dependencies require setting up too. The more it has, the more setup work for the tester.

- Tightly couple your modules. This frustrates testers' efforts at focusing on a single unit because the behavior of the other unit(s) impacts that of the unit under test.

- Create deep inheritance hierarchies. Testing a class located deep in the hierarchy requires a lot of setup work. Plus, hidden relationships and method overrides make it hard to understand a class's expected behavior.

Apply these practices as much as you can to give the testers hell.

Thumbs Down!

Earlier chapters examine all the practices cited here. They explain both why the practices are considered bad as well as more acceptable alternatives. Choosing a better alternative practice usually improves the testability of the unit.

Set Traps in Your Tests

Unit tests are supposed to live forever. Once written, they stay in the codebase, acting as vigilant verifiers of functionality and guardians against regression. After a test is incorporated into the codebase, it might seem that your opportunity to cause havoc with that test has passed.

Actually, it hasn't.

Imagine writing a unit test akin to a ticking time bomb. It initially passes and gets accepted into the codebase, but it's a trap, ready to catch an unfortunate colleague who strays too close.

It's possible to write such tests, ones that can easily break at an unknown future date for no readily apparent reason and that cause colleagues to curse your name after they've ventured into the rabbit hole of your test code.

Machine-specific Tests

"Well, it works on *my* machine."

There's a special place in hell reserved for people who use this phrase. Here's how to book your place.

It's not uncommon to find that a program works correctly on one machine but fails on another. Of course, other programmers try their best to avoid this outcome. You, however, actively seek it.

One common reason for this discrepancy is that the program references some kind of external resource whose nature differs between machines. You can use this fact to write temperamental tests, ones that initially work for you but then later break down when someone else runs them.

For example, when tests refer to resources residing on your machine (but not necessarily on others), they will work for you but fail when your colleagues run them on their own machines. The following script tests a simple food-menu program. The program reads the names of menu items in from a text file:

```java
public class Menu {
    private List<String> items = new ArrayList<>();

    public void loadMenu(String path) throws IOException {
        Path menuFile = Paths.get(path);
        BufferedReader reader =
                Files.newBufferedReader(menuFile,
                StandardCharsets.UTF_8);
        String line;
        while ((line = reader.readLine()) != null) {
            addItem(line);
        }
    }

    public void addItem(String s) {
        items.add(s);
    }

    public int getMenuSize() {
        return items.size();
    }
}
```

All fine, but your test script verifies the loadMenu method like this:

```
@Test
public void testLoadMenu() {
    Menu m = new Menu();
    // A file with 8 menu items.
    m.loadMenu(
            "c:\\Users\\asmith\\MenuApp\\data\\menuData.txt");

    assertEquals(m.getMenuSize(), 8);
}
```

That hard-coded file path points to the personal home folder on your own machine . . . a location that exists nowhere else, meaning that the test passes for you, but fails on another machine.

Admittedly, hard-coded file paths might go wrong a little too quickly and be caught by your colleagues too easily, but other more subtle techniques exist. For example, altering the previous test to use environment variables[4] can make it look as though you're writing a machine-independent test:

```
@Test
public void testLoadMenu() {
    Menu m - new Mcnu();
    String path = System.getenv("CD") +
            "\\data\\menuData.txt";
    m.loadMenu(path);

    assertEquals(m.getMenuSize(), 8);
}
```

The CD value is available on Microsoft Windows machines and holds the location of the Current Directory in which the program is being run. That means the tests should now work on any machine, so long as it's a Windows machine. Other platforms, like Linux or OS X don't support the CD environment variable (the equivalent is typically called PWD[5] in those cases). So, as soon as a Linux-loving or Apple-adulating colleague comes along, their attempts to run the test result in surprising failure.

---

[4]Named values stored by the operating system that are available to running processes.
[5]Which stands for Present Working Directory.

Thumbs Down!

Unless you want to really annoy your colleagues, every aspect about the program you're testing should be reproducible on any machine. That includes both the program and anything external on which the program depends. External resources vary depending on the environment, so they need careful control.

The previous example demonstrated file paths. When your program uses files, you need to control for the variability of a file system. Remember, you can't always make assumptions about the following:

- The location of the program on the file system (the user might have installed it anywhere)

- Which platform the program is installed on (e.g., Windows or Linux), and thus which kind of file system you're dealing with

For reasons like these, you should refer to files using platform-independent means[6] and consider using relative paths.

If your tests use environment variables, then your test-execution scripts should include setup of those variables prior to execution.

Another common problem is external dependencies, such as third-party libraries. Just because *you* have the required library on your machine, doesn't necessarily mean that everybody else does. If an external dependency is required to run your tests, then obtaining that dependency should be a quick and painless (and preferably automatic) process. Remember that identifying an external dependency can require several pieces of information, like a name *and* a version number. Otherwise, if you reference *only* the name and use features exclusive to version 3 of FooLibrary, your colleague who only has version 2 installed will encounter problems.

Expansive Focus

When a failure occurs in the test suite, one of your colleagues will be assigned the job of debugging the cause. Your colleagues no doubt insist debugging is a good thing. So, why not make a thoughtful gesture and create more debugging work for them, since they love it so much?

---

[6]For example, in Java, instead of `new Path("path/to/file.txt")` use `Paths.get("path", "to", "file.txt")`.

You can do this by expanding the scope of your unit tests beyond the behavior of the unit in question. When you involve several additional program units in a test, it can be broken by a problem in any of those extra units. That means the person debugging the failure must search more places for the problem.

For example, dispatching an online order from a customer typically involves several stages. This sample of code shows a dispatch process from a program:

```java
public class Order {
    public void dispatch()
    {
        OrderChecker checker = new OrderChecker();
        BankConnection bank = new BankConnection();

        // Only dispatch if a) the order is valid and
        // b) the funds have been received for this order.
        if (checker.validate(this) &&
            bank.fundsReceived(this.orderNumber))
        {
            // code for dispatching order
        }
    }
}

class OrderChecker {
    boolean validate(Order order) { ... }
    // etc...
}

class BankConnection {
    boolean fundsReceived(String orderNumber) { ... }
    // etc...
}
```

Observing that a test of the Order.dispatch fails is usually taken to mean an error occurred in the Order class. However, the dispatch method depends on the methods from other classes. A test for the Order.dispatch method also covers the behavior of the OrderChecker.validate and BankConnection.fundsReceived methods. This test method can be made to fail by bugs in OrderChecker or BankConnection also, giving your colleagues more code to debug.

Thumbs Down!

When writing a test, you need to be clear at which level the test focuses.

It's a perfectly valid and useful thing to test several collaborating units together, as in the previous example. These are examples of integration tests. Such tests verify that the various modules of your program function together as expected, because faults can arise when otherwise correct units are "wired" together.

However, a unit test focuses on a single unit in isolation to make sure that it works correctly before you broaden your testing scope. That way, when a bug appears in a unit, you don't have to pick apart the various collaborating modules in order to find where the bug is. A failure in the OrderTest class should imply that a bug has appeared in the Order class only.

That raises the question: how can you test a subroutine that includes calls to other modules? The answer is to take the other classes out of the equation. We can do this in two steps.

First, we adjust the program code. By instantiating the OrderChecker and BankConnection objects itself, the dispatch method has taken on additional responsibility and more tightly coupled itself to those other classes. Let's instead turn those objects into method parameters[7]:

```java
public void dispatch(OrderChecker checker,
      BankConnection bank) {
   if (checker.validate(this) &&
      bank.fundsReceived(this.orderNumber))
   {
      // code for dispatching order
   }
}
```

Second, we adjust the test code. Instead of creating real instances of OrderChecker and BankConnection, we mock them. That doesn't mean make fun of them; rather, it means we create dummy versions of them that behave in a fixed manner that you

---

[7]An alternative to using method parameters here would be to use something called dependency injection. I won't discuss it here though, so look it up yourself.

dictate. Mocking frameworks are available in many languages, and they work something like this:

```java
@Test
public void testDispatch() {
    // Create empty, 'pretend' versions of the two
    // classes.
    OrderChecker checker = MockFramework
            .createMock(OrderChecker.class);
    BankConnection bank = MockFramework
            .createMock(BankConnection.class);

    // Tell the dummy OrderChecker to return true
    // whenever the validate method is called.
    MockFramework
            .when(checker.validate())
            .thenReturn(true);

    // Tell the dummy BankConnection to return true
    // whenever the fundsReceived method is called.
    MockFramework
            .when(bank.fundsReceived())
            .thenReturn(true);

    Order testOrder = createNewOrder();
    testOrder.dispatch(checker, bank);
    assertTrue(order.isDispatched());
}
```

Now that the behavior of the other classes is taken out of consideration, this test depends solely on the Order class's behavior.

Chaos

Programming is all about control. It's like playing with the biggest, most complex train set imaginable, and so it requires the most careful coordination among all elements. Every event should trigger on schedule and every object should be in its required state from moment to moment. Making a program predictable makes it testable.

Reducing predictability therefore makes code less testable. To reduce the predictability of your program, you can introduce non-determinism into the mix. A non-deterministic routine is one whose output can vary given the same inputs. While you can control the production of the output, you can't control what that output is.

A good example of this is randomness. You can generate a random number whenever you wish, but the *result* is, by definition, beyond your control. This compromises the testability of code that depends on randomness.

For example, you can't test a specific value:

```
@Test
public void testDiceThrow() {
    int result = DiceThrow.getNextThrow();

    // Roughly 5 out of 6 times, this test would fail.
    assertTrue(result == 2);
}
```

But you can test that a valid result is returned:

```
@Test
public void testDiceThrow() {
    int result = DiceThrow.getNextThrow();

    assertTrue(result <= 6);
}
```

You can take advantage of this imprecision to smuggle in a problem or two. One way to do it could be to sneak a bug into the program code:

```
public class DiceThrow {
    public static int getNextThrow() {
        Random rand = new Random();
        return rand.nextInt(6);
    }
}
```

Java's Random.nextInt(n) method returns a random number between 0 inclusively and n *exclusively*. This means our getNextThrow method will only ever return numbers between 0 and 5. However, our reasonable-looking test is actually flawed because it will never expose that problem.

184

You could also have a bit of fun by smuggling an extra problem into the test code by adjusting the assertion slightly:

```
@Test
public void testDiceThrow() {
    int result = DiceThrow.getNextThrow();

    assertTrue(result >= 1 && result <= 6);
}
```

Now, the test will occasionally fail (roughly 17 percent of the time, on those occasions when getNextThrow returns 0), causing confusion all round as different people on your team get different test results from test run to test run.

It's not only randomness that results in volatility. Time can also be problematic. Let's say you have some kind of sales program with a happy-hour feature (products sold at a certain time are subject to a discount):

```
public class Product {
    private int price;

    public Product(int price) {
        this.price = price;
    }

    public int getPrice() {
        LocalDateTime now = LocalDateTime.now();
        // Sales between midnight and 1am are half off
        if (now.getHour() >= 0 && now.getHour() < 1) {
            return price / 2;
        }
        return price;
    }
}
```

And you test the product like this:

```
@Test
public void testGetPrice() {
    // Create a product priced at $10.00
    Product p = new Product(1000);
    int price = p.getPrice();

    assertTrue(Integer.toString(price), price == 1000);
}
```

Most of the time, this test will pass. But anyone who's burning the midnight oil might think they're dreaming when tests suddenly start failing around the stroke of midnight.

Even better, many projects institute automatic nightly builds that compile the code and run all the tests around midnight. This means your teammates will turn up for work the next day to find reports of a failing test that ran overnight.[8] However, when they run the tests themselves, they'll discover that everything in the test suite passes fine.

Even betterer, if the build takes a long time (more than an hour), testGetPrice might sometimes be run during happy hour and sometimes outside of it, resulting in a phantom bug that appears on one night and disappears the next.

Thumbs Down!

It's considered very bad form for test suites to flip randomly between passing and failing. You should isolate the volatile parts of a test and bring them under your control.

That might mean altering the program code itself. The Product.getPrice example is a good instance of this. Its design could be improved to make it more testable, specifically by making the current time a parameter to the method:

```
public int getPrice(LocalDateTime now) {
    // Sales between midnight and 1am are half off
    if (now.getHour() >= 0 && now.getHour() < 1) {
        return price / 2;
    }
    return price;
}
```

---

[8]The testGetPrice method fails around midnight because the price expected by the test is not what getPrice returns at this time.

This way, you can create LocalDateTime objects set to a time of your own choosing:

```
@Test
public void testGetPriceAtMidnight() {
    Product p = new Product(1000);

    // 10 Jan 2017, 00:00
    LocalDateTime midnight = LocalDateTime.of(
            2017, Month.JANUARY, 10, 00, 00);
    int price = p.getPrice(midnight);

    assertTrue(Integer.toString(price), price == 500);
}
```

External dependencies with a mind of their own (like I/O or network connections) can also be problematic. If your program code makes use of one during a test, its volatility can also affect the result. For example, the sales program might consult a networked server to ensure each product's price is up-to-date:

```
public class Product {
    private int price;

    public void checkPrice(Server priceServer) {
        QueryResponse response -
                priceServer.getPrice(p);
        if (response.getPrice() != this.price) {
            System.out.println("Updating price.");
            this.price = response.getPrice();
        }
    }
    // etc...
}
```

The aim of testing the Product.checkPrice method would be to ensure that the price is adjusted correctly if necessary, but the price server's availability becomes an unwanted factor in the test. For instance, if the server is unavailable at the moment of testing, the test will fail.

In a case like this, you could apply the same solution from the previous section: object mocking. In the real sales program, an *actual* Server object represents a connection to a real networked machine and can be large and complex. During a test, a *mocked* Server object needs only be a pretend server, programmed to provide a fixed response that you dictate.

```
@Test
public void testCheckPrice() {
    Product p = new Product(1000);

    // priceServer is an empty, 'pretend' Server
    Server priceServer =
            MockFramework.createMock(Server.class);

    // Tell priceServer to return 900 whenever
    // getPrice method is called
    MockFramework
            .when(priceServer.getPrice())
            .thenReturn(900);

    p.checkPrice(priceServer);
    assertEquals(product.getPrice(), 900);
}
```

Again, this brings a volatile part of the test under your control.

CHAPTER 11

Debugging

Objectives

In this chapter, you'll learn:

- How to carry out debugging as an incompetently led investigation, specifically by:

    - Making wild guesses

    - Favoring your own pet theories

    - Refusing to be methodical

- How to frustrate debugging by writing code that leaves no clues behind

- How to avoid carrying out proper fixes on faulty code

Prerequisites

Before reading this chapter, make sure you're familiar with debuggers and their basic facilities, like stepping through code and inspecting variables.

Introduction

You can't win them all. Not every bug you create will escape the attention of your conscientious colleagues. When this happens, they will drag you back to the IDE and force debugging upon you.

It's not all sad news, however. Just like other areas of programming, debugging can be approached in a number of different ways, some good, some bad. You may sometimes have to debug, but you don't have to do it *well*.

189

© Karl Beecher 2018
K. Beecher, *Bad Programming Practices 101*, https://doi.org/10.1007/978-1-4842-3411-2_11

Investigate Unsystematically

Debugging bears an uncanny resemblance to detective work, except the crime is that someone wrote a bug. No one knows the exact circumstances, so it's necessary to investigate and find out precisely what happened, as well as where and when.

Naturally, you'd prefer not to investigate. If you've been following the advice in this book, the chances are good that *you're* the culprit. Still, it would raise too much suspicion if you didn't at least appear to investigate. And how often does the criminal get to investigate his own crime?

The world's most celebrated detective, Sherlock Holmes, left behind a collection of great advice in his stories. Thanks to its logical and methodical nature, his crime-fighting guidance also applies very well to bug-hunting. But you won't be emulating Holmes. That would be far too successful a strategy. Instead, take inspiration from those other characters, the bumbling bobbies of Scotland Yard, whom the Great Detective often bewilders and antagonizes.

In other words, don't be like Holmes; be like Inspector Lestrade.

Guesswork

I never guess. It is a shocking habit, — destructive to the logical faculty.

—The Sign of Four

Real-world programs are often large beasts, thousands of lines long, sometimes millions. You surely have no hope of finding that needle of a bug inside such a haystack of code. But you have to look somewhere, so you might as well guess.

Do the equivalent of banging a faulty machine with a wrench. Pick some random spots in the code and play about with them to see what happens: throw in some `print` statements to see if they're triggered unexpectedly, then tweak a few lines of code to see whether that gets rid of the problem.

If you're unlucky, you'll stumble upon the bug eventually. However, if you're lucky, you'll run out of time and be left with a trampled codebase full of `print` statements and hastily tweaked code.

Thumbs Down!

The first step in an investigation is to search for clues. You should then use these to form a hypothesis, which is a sort of guess. However, a hypothesis distinguishes itself from mere guesswork in several respects. In particular, a hypothesis:

1. Is testable and therefore falsifiable

2. Is based on observations as opposed to being plucked out of the air

3. Should fit with existing knowledge

4. Shouldn't require making lots of assumptions and therefore tends to be simple[1]

A programmer who's debugging acts akin to a detective, albeit a detective who can travel in time. By running the program and triggering the error, you can re-run what happened at the "scene of the crime" repeatedly until you determine the steps that caused the error. In this sense, debugging more strongly resembles a scientific investigation rather than a criminal one.

Like a scientist, you're trying to link a cause (the mistake in the code) with an effect (the error). After repeated executions, you might establish that the error only seems to occur when you, for example, load a file whose name contains whitespace, or when you submit a form without first selecting one of gender radio buttons.

Once you can reliably reproduce the error at will, you can proceed to the next stage, which is to find precisely what's causing things to going wrong.

Biases

It is a capital mistake to theorize before one has data. Insensibly one begins to twist facts to suit theories, instead of theories to suit facts.

—A Scandal in Bohemia

You should identify yourself strongly with every belief you hold. Attach your pride to them. The stronger you identify yourself with a belief, the truer it will be. You'll know that this identification is strong enough when you feel personal offense as soon as anyone expresses opposition to your beliefs.

---

[1]This is based on the principle of Occam's Razor.

It's good to bring this attitude specifically to debugging. Upon discovery of an error, you should rush to a conclusion (preferably one that is exotic and complicated) and adopt that as your pet theory. From there on in, you should start searching only for evidence that confirms your theory.

Defend your belief as though your ego depended on it. If new facts begin to make your theory look tenuous, try to twist and reinterpret the facts until they accommodate it better. If you discover facts that rule out your theory entirely, just ignore them.

Thumbs Down!

An ego is a dangerous thing to possess during an investigation.

True, Sherlock Holmes displayed some breathtaking egotism himself, but he attached his ego to the successful resolution of cases, not to the explanations themselves. Holmes's mind worked ruthlessly through dozens of theories during an investigation: forming them, comparing each to the known facts, and discarding it the moment it contradicted reality.

You, too, should be ruthless with every hypothesis you form. When beginning to debug, you have only partial information, so your hypothesis will be tentative. Later, as you gather more information, your initial hypothesis may not fit with those new facts. At this point, you have two options:

1. Adjust the hypothesis to explain the additional facts (making sure it still fits the existing ones).

2. Discard the hypothesis if a fact rules it out entirely, and form a new hypothesis.

Neither choice means any reason to be ashamed. Even experienced, professional programmers rarely see their earliest theory survive investigation unscathed.

Chaos

> . . . when you have excluded the impossible, whatever remains, however improbable, must be the truth.
>
> —The Beryl Coronet

When you're hunting a bug, it can happen that your actions cause the error during one execution, but seemingly don't cause that error during another identical execution.

What's happening? Well, obviously . . . um . . . *bugs move around!* So cunning must they be, these critters clearly know you're searching for them, so they hop around your program from module to module, trying to evade you.

If we believe that bugs are mobile, the nature of debugging changes. You can say goodbye to an orderly, methodical investigation. Instead, it becomes a fevered chase. You can jump from place to place in search of the problem. You can eschew looking for any patterns at all. You can even change the code in several places at once in an effort to attack the bug from multiple sides.

Thumbs Down!

Bugs don't move around, despite occasional appearances to the contrary. A bug is not a conscious creature; it's a mistake in the code. It no more moves around a program than a plot hole moves around the pages of a novel.

That means you can (and should) be methodical in finding the source of an error. There are numerous debugging tips and strategies you can follow, but this section introduces a few of the most pertinent.

First, you should be aware of certain well-established patterns that suggest likely hiding places for bugs. For example:

- Complex code tends to harbor more bugs than simple code (this was discussed in several earlier chapters).

- Volatile code (i.e., code that gets changed often) tends to harbor more bugs than stable code.

- Newer code tends to harbor more bugs than older code because the older stuff has been used and tested more.

Being conscious of these patterns gives you reasons to prioritize certain areas of the program above others when looking for sources of errors.

In addition, you can take advantage the classic strategy "divide and conquer," which advocates breaking up a target into pieces and dealing with each one separately. When debugging, your target is the codebase, and dealing with a piece means eliminating it as a potential source of error. You can start with a wide scope, then repeatedly eliminate parts of the program chunk by chunk until the scope is narrowed right down to the defective lines of code.

For example, if you observe that a variable has an incorrect value at a certain point during execution, then

- this point becomes the latter boundary of suspicious code, since the variable took on its value at this point *at the latest*; and

- the initialization of the variable become the earliest boundary.

All code executed between these boundaries falls under suspicion. You can then inspect the value at some midway point, which eliminates from suspicion all code executed before that point (if the value is still correct) or after that point (if the value is already incorrect). After adjusting the boundaries accordingly, you now have an area of code roughly half the size, from which you can then choose another midway point and repeat the process.

Finally, it can help during debugging to tweak a little bit of code here and there. ("Does it still fail if I change it to *this* value?") If you choose to do that, stick to changing *one thing at a time*, even if you have several ideas you want to try. This is a lesson any scientist could teach you. The scientist conducting an experiment, searching for the cause of a specific effect, varies the independent variable (i.e., the input) to see its effect on the dependent variable (i.e., the observed output). If they tweak several inputs all at once and observe an effect, how do they know which of the inputs was truly the cause? The same logic applies to debugging.

Make Debugging Hard

Good criminals cover their tracks and make detection of their crimes hard. The great ones make it hard to determine a crime was even committed at all.

You're not a criminal, but you could learn a thing or two from talented lawbreakers. Take some inspiration from them and make it harder for your fellow programmers to track down your bugs.

Always Keep Your Mouth Shut

If a program messes up, the last thing it should do is admit to the user that the fault lies with the program. However, if you ensure that a program fouls up without warning or explanation, you might succeed in surreptitiously convincing the user it was all their fault.

Think about it: if a program helpfully explains a problem, the user will know that the program did something wrong. But if it unexpectedly dies in the middle of a session for no discernible reason, the clueless user is more likely to sit there, wide-eyed, exclaiming, "What did I do wrong?" Did you see the subtle shift in blame, there?

Besides, what good can arise from listening to the nonsensical ramblings of a faulty program? Anything it says is probably meaningless, right?

Thumbs Down!

When a program fails, that usually means it tried to execute an invalid instruction. That doesn't mean the computer suddenly lost its mind and that nothing it reports can be trusted.

You should be honest and upfront about failure. As soon as an error threatens to derail the program in some way, inform the user. As Chapter 7 explained,[2] this should be a message that assumes no technical skill on their part but is nevertheless helpful and informative.

Furthermore, you should provide information about the failure for the program's author too. That can include:

- A stack trace, which is very helpful for telling you

  - in which subroutine (and maybe at which specific instruction) the program failed, which hints at the location of the bug; and

  - which series of subroutine calls had been executed at the point of failure, which can help reconstruct the series of events leading to the failure.

- The generated error message, such as the contents of `Exception.getMessage()` in Java programs.

- Important values like

  - program version;

  - date and time; and

  - any relevant variables or other objects at the time of failure.

The technical stuff will have to be kept aside for the programmer to look at later. More on that in the following subsection.

---

[2]See the section "Send Problems Down the Memory Hole."

Keeping Records

If your colleagues insist on the program reporting error data, then all this debugging information has to be conveyed somehow. The question is: how?

Obviously, you should just use a normal `print` statement. What could be simpler for you? All you have to do is add them to your code at the points where significant events should be reported. But there are other advantages to using `print` statements that should suit your malevolent outlook on life.

For one thing, debugging information presented using `print` statements is always switched on. For text-based programs, that adds additional noise to the output, which distracts and frustrates the user (which is always a good thing to do). If your colleagues want to remove that noise, they'll have to slog through all the code, finding and removing your offending `print` statements.

Alternatively, if your program is GUI-based, then the debug output will be invisible to the user. In fact, it will be invisible to just about everybody, including the programmer, who would desperately want to see it in the event of an error. However, since ordinary print output doesn't get recorded anywhere, that precious debug information vanishes long before news of a bug reaches the programmer.

Thumbs Down!

Nobody is going to object to your adding `print` statements temporarily to your own copy of the code. What you get up to in your own repository is your own business. But once you finally commit your changes to the canonical version of the program, any "temporary" `print` statements must come out.

An alternative means to outputting debug information is logging. Most programming languages provide built-in means to do this nowadays, and it can safely be put into the production version of a program. For example, here's a simple way to set up logging in a Java class:

```java
import java.util.logging.Logger;

public class Main {

    private final Logger log =
            Logger.getLogger(Main.class.getName());
```

```
public void makeRequest(Network network) {
    log.info("Making request to remote server: " +
            network.getServerName());

    if (network.getStatus() ==
            NetStat.UNAVAILABLE) {
        log.warning("Network is unavailable.");
    }

    // etc...
    }
}
```

This makes the class Main available for logging. By making calls to the Logger object, you can record a log message. They look something like this:

```
Oct 21, 2015 4:26:35 PM Main makeRequest
INFO: Making request to remote server: ulysses
Oct 21, 2015 4:26:37 PM Main makeRequest
WARNING: Network is unavailable.
```

Logs give you much greater control over your debug output than print statements do. A key feature is the ability to direct log information to a variety of different destinations. A Java logger outputs to the console by default, but you could also make it record the message to a file:

```
public class Main {

    private static final Logger log =
            Logger.getLogger(Main.class.getName());

    private Handler fileHandler = null;

    public Main() {
        fileHandler = new FileHandler("log.txt");
        log.addHandler(fileHandler);
    }

    public void makeRequest() {
        // This method remains unchanged...
```

Another feature is log levels. These allow you to assign each log message a severity. You could then instruct the program to output only the messages of a certain minimum severity or above, or direct messages of a different severity to different log files. Typical levels in ascending order of severity include the following:

- Debug/Trace: Intended for messages that are useful when you're debugging and want to carefully trace what happened (e.g., outputting an object's value or indicating that a method just began executing)

- Info: For messages describing notable events (e.g., new customer added to the system, incoming network request)

- Warn: For unexpected events that, while they don't prevent the program from running, might indicate problems (e.g., low memory, logon failed)

- Error: For messages describing occasions when the program couldn't function properly (e.g., tried to update a record in the database but failed)

- Fatal: For events that cause the application to fail (e.g., out of memory)

Avoid Proper Fixes

The aim of debugging is ultimately to find and repair the bug. But there's more than one way this story can end . . .

The Hit 'n' Run Bug

Software in execution is chaotic, complex stuff, what with all those millions of bits flipping values billions of times per second in perfect synchronicity. It's a wonder programs ever function correctly at all. So, why should anyone be surprised that, in among the chaos, a hit 'n' run bug occurs now and again. Most experienced software developers know what I mean by this.

The story usually goes like this: One day, you encounter a weird error during an execution of the program. Dutifully, you try to reproduce the bug, running the program once more and performing the same steps again only to find that everything worked fine the second time. Even after several more executions, the error can't be coaxed into reappearing.

Other programmers might let something like this worry them, but not you. You know that random problems like this are bound to occur now and again, given how thoroughly complex software is. The bug responsible probably disappeared immediately anyway and so isn't worth worrying about.

Thumbs Down!

I'm sorry to be a bore, but if an error occurred in your program and the code hasn't been altered since, the bug responsible is most definitely still there. You might have been unable to reproduce the problem so far, but that only means you haven't determined the exact conditions that trigger it.

It may be true that the bug caused only a slight problem,[3] and so fixing it isn't an urgent matter—that's a different discussion—but you can't say that the bug no longer exists. At the very least, the error needs recording in your project's bug database.

You do have one of those . . . don't you?

Patch It Up

Unfortunately, things may reach the point where a fix for a bug is demanded. However, you don't necessarily have to give in and repair things just yet. You might have done your best so far to thwart debugging efforts—such as by sabotaging the investigation and writing hard-to-debug code—but you still have another trick up your sleeve to help preserve the bug—a technique that makes it only *appear* as though you fixed something. We have the medical profession to thank for it.

Some doctors make an effort to heal ailments. Others are happy to merely treat the symptoms, leaving the underlying problem untouched. You can learn from this latter group of medics, because you can view fixing bugs in similar terms. Take this code, for example, which calculates student grades from their scores:

```
// Grade is between A and F inclusively
String grade = calculateGrade(student.getTestScore());
System.out.println(grade);
```

---

[3]Or, to put it more technically, the error had a low severity.

It contains a problem: the variable grade occasionally ends up with the value null. That should never happen, and the job of fixing the problem falls to you. As a minimal effort, you look at the list of scores and find which ones cause calculateGrade to return null.

```
45 -> "E"
67 -> "C"
68 -> "C"
81 -> "A"
40 -> null
73 -> "B"
```

The only problem you identify is that scores of exactly 40 return null when they should equate to a grade "F."

So, the calculateGrade subroutine seems to contain an underlying problem. A symptom of this is that your calling code prints out an incorrect value whenever the score is 40. You now have a choice. Do you fix the symptom or the underlying problem?

Fixing the underlying problem involves a lot of work: diving into the calculateGrade routine, analyzing the code, forming a hypothesis to explain the bug, coming up with ways to test that hypothesis, perhaps writing some new tests to make sure the bug was fixed.

On the other hand, fixing the symptom is comparatively easy:

```
// Grade is between A and F inclusively
String grade;
if (student.getTestScore() == 40) {
    grade = "F";
}
else {
    grade = calculateGrade(student.getTestScore());
}
System.out.println(grade);
```

When you run the program again, all scores in the test data now result in the correct grade. Like any remedy that treats only a symptom, the problem is fixed superficially.

If you find words like "easy" and "superficial" very appealing, as I'm sure you do, you should favor the symptom-based approach to healing.

Thumbs Down!

Fixing the symptom is not automatically a bad thing. Occasionally, it's your only option; for example, if you're using a third-party library for which you don't have the source code. However, failing to even try to fix the underlying problem when you *do* have the opportunity is poor practice.

Focusing on the symptom means the underlying problem remains. In the previous example, we may have patched up one call to the problematic subroutine, but what if another call to the subroutine gets added later? Naturally, the bug will resurface.

What's more, failing to look into `calculateGrade` means you can't be sure of understanding the actual problem. In the previous example, a single hypothesis was formed that happened to fit with one of the observed facts, but it was not then investigated further. If you had examined that subroutine, you might have seen the problem in more detail:

```
public String calculateGrade(int score) {
    String grade = null;

    if (score > 80) { grade = "A"; }
    else if (score > 70) { grade = "B"; }
    else if (score > 60) { grade = "C"; }
    else if (score > 50) { grade = "D"; }
    else if (score > 40) { grade = "E"; }
    else if (score < 40) { grade = "E"; }

    return grade;
}
```

None of the clauses in the `if` statement account for scores of 40, so `calculateGrade` returns null in this case.

However, the code also contains another mistake: the last clause in the `if` statement returns a grade of "E" instead of "F." Since none of the original test data contained any values lower than 40, this specific bug wasn't exposed; thus, your fix of the symptom doesn't take it into account.

A proper analysis of the code would have led to a genuine resolution of the bug by altering the last clause to this:

```
    else if (score <= 40) { grade = "F"; }
```

Bibliography

Apple. 2013. *Code Naming Basics*. Accessed 07 Sep 2017, `https://developer.apple.com/library/content/documentation/Cocoa/Conceptual/CodingGuidelines/Articles/NamingBasics.html`.

Basili, V.R., and B.T. Perricone. 1984. "Software Errors and Complexity: An Empirical Investigation," *Communications of the ACM*, 27(1): 42-52.

Basili, V.R., L. Briand, and W.L. Melo. 1996. "A Validation of Object-oriented Design Metrics as Quality Indicators," *IEEE Transactions on Software Engineering*, October, 22(10), 751–761.

Bezier, B. 1990. *Software Testing Techniques*. Van Nostrand Reinhold, New York.

Bloch, J. 2008. *Effective Java: Programming Language Guide, Second Edition*. Prentice Hall PTR, Upper Saddle River, NJ, USA.

Briand, L.C., and J. Wüst. 2002. "Empirical Studies of Quality Models in Object-oriented Systems," *Advances in Computers*, 56: 97-166.

Brooks, F.P. 1995. *The Mythical Man-Month*. Addison-Wesley, Boston, MA, USA.

CA/CST/Systems Integration & Innovation Division (CA-CST-SII). 2015. *C Coding Standards*. Available at: `https://github.com/CA-CST-SII/Software-Standards/wiki/C---Coding-Standards`. Last updated: 11 Feb 2015.

Card, David N., Victor E. Church, and William W. Agresti. "An Empirical Study of Software Design Practices," *IEEE Transactions on Software Engineering*, 2(1986): 264-271.

Chidamber, S.R., and C.F. Kemerer. 1994. "A Metrics Suite for Object-oriented Design," *IEEE Transactions on Software Engineering*, 20(6): 476-493.

Cypher, A., Dontcheva, M., Lau, T., and Nichols, J. 2010. No code required: giving users tools to transform the web. Morgan Kaufmann.

Dunlosky, J., K.A. Rawson, E.J. Marsh, M.J. Nathan, and D.T. Willingham. 2013. "Improving Students' Learning with Effective Learning Techniques: Promising Directions from Cognitive and Educational Psychology," *Psychological Science in the Public Interest*, 14(1): 4-58.

© Karl Beecher 2018
K. Beecher, *Bad Programming Practices 101*, https://doi.org/10.1007/978-1-4842-3411-2

BIBLIOGRAPHY

Dijkstra, E.W. 1968. "Letters to the Editor: Go To Statement Considered Harmful," *Communications of the ACM*, 11(3): 147-148.

Elshoff, J.L. 1976. "An Analysis of Some Commercial PL/I Programs," *IEEE Transactions on Software Engineering*, (2): 113-120.

Endres, A., and D. Rombach. 2003. *A Handbook of Software and Systems Engineering: Empirical Observations. Laws and Theories*. Addison-Wesley, Harlow, England; New York.

ESA Board for Software Standardisation and Control. 2004. *Java Coding Standards*. Technical report.

Fowler, M. 1999. *Refactoring: Improving the Design of Existing Code*. Addison-Wesley Professional, Boston, MA, USA.

Gamma, E., R. Helm, R. Johnson, and J. Vlissides. 1995. *Design Patterns: Elements of Reusable Object-Oriented Software*. Addison-Wesley, Boston, MA, USA.

Glass, R.L. 2002. *Facts and Fallacies of Software Engineering*. Addison-Wesley Professional, Boston, MA, USA.

Google. 2017a. *Google C++ Style Guide*. Accessed 07 Sep 2017, `https://google.github.io/styleguide/cppguide.html`.

-----. 2017b. Google Java Style Guide. Accessed 07 Sep 2017, `https://google.github.io/styleguide/javaguide.html`.

Gorla, N., A.C. Benander, and B.A. Benander, B.A. 1990. "Debugging Effort Estimation Using Software Metrics," *IEEE Transactions on Software Engineering*, 16(2): 223-231.

GNU. 2016. *GNU Coding Standards*. Web page. Accessed 07 Sep 2017, `https://www.gnu.org/prep/standards/standards.html`.

Gyimothy, T., R. Ferenc, and I. Siket. 2005. "Empirical Validation of Object-oriented Metrics on Open Source Software for Fault Prediction," *IEEE Transactions on Software Engineering*, 31(10): 897-910.

Hoare, T. 2009. *Null References: The Billion Dollar Mistake*. Accessed 07 Sep 2017, `https://qconlondon.com/london-2009/qconlondon.com/london-2009/index.html`.

Johnson, R.E., and B. Foote. 1988. "Designing Reusable Classes," *Journal of Object-oriented Programming*, 1(2): 22-35.

JPL, 2009. *JPL Institutional Coding Standard for the C Programming Language*. California Institute of Technology. Technical report.

Kappelman, L.A., R. McKeeman, and L. Zhang. 2006. "Early Warning Signs of IT Project Failure: The Dominant Dozen," *Information systems management*, 23(4): 31-36.

Kemeny, J.G., and T.E. Kurtz. 1964. *BASIC Instruction Manual*. Dartmouth College: Hanover, NH.

Kernel.org, 2017. *Kernel Coding Style*. Available from: `http://lxr.linux.no/` `linux+v4.10.1/Documentation/process/coding-style.rst`.

Kernighan, B.W., and P.J. Plauger. 1978. *The Elements of Programming Style*. McGraw-Hill, New York, NY, USA.

Keil, M., P.E. Cule, K. Lyytinen, and R.C. Schmidt. 1998. "A framework for identifying software project risks," *Communications of the ACM*, 41(11): 76-83.

Lahtinen, E., K. Ala-Mutka, and H.M. Järvinen. 2005, June. "A Study of the Difficulties of Novice Programmers," *ACIM SIGCSE Bulletin* 37(3): 14-18. ACM.

Lind, R.K., and K. Vairavan. 1989. "An Experimental Investigation of Software Metrics and Their Relationship to Software Development Effort," *IEEE Transactions on Software Engineering*, 15(5): 649-653.

Long, F., D. Mohindra, R.C. Seacord, D.F. Sutherland, and D. Svoboda, D. 2013. *Java Coding Guidelines: 75 Recommendations for Reliable and Secure Programs*. Addison-Wesley.

Martin, R.C. 1996. "The Liskov Substitution Principle," *C++ Report*, 8(3): 14.

------. 2009. *Clean Code: A Handbook of Agile Software Craftsmanship*. Prentice-Hall, Upper Saddle River, NJ, USA.

McCabe, T.J. 1976. "A Complexity Measure," *IEEE Transactions on software Engineering*, (4): 308-320.

McConnell, S. 2004. *Code Complete, Second Edition*. Microsoft Press, Redmond, WA, USA.

Miara, R.J., J.A. Musselman, J.A. Navarro, and B. Shneiderman. 1983. "Program Indentation and Comprehensibility," *Communications of the ACM*, 26(11): 861-867.

Microsoft. 2016. *CA1501: Avoid Excessive Inheritance*. Accessed 07 Nov 2017. `https://docs.microsoft.com/en-us/visualstudio/code-quality/` `ca1501-avoid-excessive-inheritance`.

------. 2017. *Best Practices for Exceptions*. Accessed 06 Oct 2017. `https://docs.micro-` `soft.com/en-us/dotnet/standard/exceptions/best-practices-for-exceptions`.

Mozilla. 2017. *Coding Style*. Accessed 11 Oct 2017. `https://developer.mozilla.org/` `en-US/docs/Mozilla/Developer_guide/Coding_Style`.

Mughal, K.A., T. Hamre, and R.W. Rasmussen. 2007. *Java Actually: A First Course in Programming*. Cengage Learning EMEA, London.

National Weather Service, Office of Hydrologic Development. 2007. *General Software Development Standards and Guidelines Version 3.5*. Technical report, 2007.

Oracle. 1999. *Code Conventions for the Java Programming Language*. Accessed 07 Sep 2017, `http://www.oracle.com/technetwork/articles/javase/codeconvtoc-136057.html`.

-----. 2014. *Java 8's New Type Annotations*. Accessed 07 Sep 2017, `https://blogs.oracle.com/java-platform-group/java-8s-new-type-annotations`.

-----. 2017. *Project Jigsaw*. Accessed 17 Nov 2017, `http://openjdk.java.net/projects/jigsaw`.

Orwell, G. 1949. *Nineteen Eighty-Four*. Penguin Books, London.

Pane, J.F., and B.A. Myers. 2001. "Studying the Language and Structure in Non-programmers' Solutions to Programming Problems," *International Journal of Human-Computer Studies*, 54(2): 237-264.

Papert, S. 1996. "An Exploration in the Space of Mathematics Educations," *International Journal of Computers for Mathematical Learning*, 1(1): 95-123.

Pennington, N. 1987. Stimulus structures and mental representations in expert comprehension of computer programs. *Cognitive psychology*, 19(3): 295-341.

Perlis, A.J. 1982. "Epigrams on Programming," *SIgPLAN Notices*, 17(9): 7-13.

Powers, K., P. Gross, S. Cooper, M. McNally, K.J. Goldman, V. Proulx, and M. Carlisle. 2006, March. "Tools for Teaching Introductory Programming: What Works?" *ACM SIGCSE Bulletin* 38(1): 560-561. ACM.

Pólya, G. 1973. *How to Solve It (Second Edition)*. Princeton, NJ: Princeton University Press.

Prechelt, L., B. Unger, M. Philippsen, and W. Tichy. 2003. "A Controlled Experiment on Inheritance Depth as a Cost Factor for Code Maintenance," *Journal of Systems and Software*, 65(2): 115-126.

Python. 2013. *PEP 8—Style Guide for Python Code*. Accessed 11 Oct 2017, `https://www.python.org/dev/peps/pep-0008`.

de Saint-Exupéry, A., and R. Williamson, R. 1939. *Wind, Sand, and Stars*. Penguin, London.

Selby, R.W., and V.R. Basili. 1991. "Analyzing Error-prone System Structure," *IEEE Transactions on Software Engineering*, 17(2): 141-152.

Shneiderman, B., and R. Mayer. 1979. "Syntactic/semantic Interactions in Programmer Behavior: A Model and Experimental Results," *International Journal of Parallel Programming*, 8(3): 219-238.

Tan, S.H., D. Marinov, L. Tan, and G.T. Leavens. 2012, April. *@ tcomment: Testing javadoc comments to detect comment-code inconsistencies*. In Software Testing, Verification and Validation (ICST), 2012 IEEE Fifth International Conference on (pp. 260-269). IEEE.

Tang, M.H., M.H. Kao, and M.H. Chen. 1999. *An Empirical Study on Object-oriented Metrics*. In Software Metrics Symposium, 1999. Proceedings. Sixth International (pp. 242-249). IEEE.

Turing, A.M. 1937. "On computable numbers, with an application to the Entscheidungsproblem," *Proceedings of the London Mathematical Society*, 2(1): 230-265.

Van De Vanter, M.L. 2002. "The Documentary Structure of Source Code," *Information and Software Technology*, 44(13): 767-782.

Watson, A.H., and T.J. McCabe. 1996. *Structured Testing: A Testing Methodology Using the Cyclomatic Complexity Metric*. NIST Special Publication 500-235.

Wheeler, D., 2014. *The Apple goto Fail Vulnerability: Lessons Learned*. Available at `https://www.dwheeler.com/essays/apple-goto-fail.html`. Published 23 Nov.

Yourdon, E., and L. Constantine. 1978. *Structured Design: Fundamentals Discipline of Computer Programs and System Design*. Yourdon Press, Upper Saddle River, NJ.

Yourdon, E. 1986. *Managing the Structured Techniques*. Prentice-Hall, Upper Saddle River, NJ.

Glossary

Abstract class: A class with at least one abstract method (i.e., a method declared without an implementation).

Application programming interface (API): Set of standardized methods of for building an application.

Argument (a.k.a. actual parameter): Data item supplied to a subroutine as part of a call.

Black-box testing: Testing technique that assumes the internal details of a unit are hidden.

Block: Group of program statements treated as a single unit.

Bug: Mistake in program code that causes errors.

Class: Template specifying the methods and properties for a group of similar objects.

Collection: Data structure that stores other objects.

Composition: Means of combining simple objects into more complex ones.

Conditional: Programming construct allowing the programmer to choose between actions based on the result of a Boolean condition.

Constructor: Special method of a class called whenever a new object of that class is instantiated.

Declaration: Construct that specifies the properties of something in a program, such as a variable or a subroutine.

Dependency: Relationship that includes one object using another.

Design pattern: Reusable solution form to a commonly occurring problem in software design.

Dialog: Window that appears in a GUI program when information about a choice is required or when options have to be selected.

Encapsulation: Restriction of access to technical details of a module behind an interface.

Enumeration: Defined collection of values.

Error: Fault in a running program that causes the program to produce erroneous results or to cease functioning.

Exception: Anomalous event encountered in a running program requiring special handling.

209

© Karl Beecher 2018
K. Beecher, *Bad Programming Practices 101*, https://doi.org/10.1007/978-1-4842-3411-2

Expression: Combination of values, variables, operators, and subroutine calls that is evaluated to produce a result.

Field: Individual piece of data belonging to a larger object.

Functional programming: Programming paradigm emphasizing the evaluation of mathematical-style functions and avoiding mutable state.

Goto: Unconditional jump to another point in the program.

Guard clause: Boolean expression used to evaluate whether execution of a subroutine should continue.

Graphical user interface (GUI): Means of interacting with a program emphasizing use of windows, icons, and a mouse pointer.

Integrated development environment (IDE): Program that performs the various stages of software design and implementation in a single integrated system.

If ladder: If statement made up of a series of if-else clauses.

Inheritance: Means by which the properties and methods from a parent class are made available to the inheriting class.

Initialization: Process of assigning a first value to a variable.

Instantiation: Process of creating a new object.

Input/Output (I/O): Communication between a program and the outside world.

Member: Variable (data member) or subroutine (member function) associated with an object.

Mock object: Dummy object that mimics a real object in a controlled way.

Mod (modulo operator): Operation that returns the remainder of a division.

Mutable object: Object whose value can be changed after creation (in contrast to an immutable object).

Nesting: Organizing code into layers so that constructs are contained within other constructs.

Non-deterministic: Able to produce different results on each execution.

Object: Group of data and associated program routines used within an object-oriented program.

Parameter: Local variable that takes on the value passed via an argument in a subroutine call.

Polymorphism: Provision of a single interface for communicating with many different types.

Primitive type: Basic, built-in type provided by a programming language; often value types.

Query: Request for information made to a database or other information system.

Reference type: Type of variable that stores a location in the memory allocated to it. That location refers to the place where the variable's actual value is stored.

Regression: Appearance of a bug that was absent in a previous version of the program.

Resource: Entity of limited availability (e.g., memory, disk, network).

Scope: Range of statements for which a variable is valid.

Side effect: Observable effect of calling a subroutine outside of its usual return value.

Stack trace: List of unfinished method calls made from the program's start to the point where a problem was encountered.

Subroutine: Sequence of program instructions that perform a specific task, packaged as a unit.

Type: Classification of data that makes explicit how the data may be used.

Unit test: Code fragment that verifies the functionality of a unit of code.

Uniform Resource Identifier/Locator (URI/URL): String used to identify a resource on a network.

Value type: Type of variable that stores its value directly in the memory allocated to it.

White-box testing: Testing technique that assumes the internal details of a unit are visible.

Wildcard: Symbol used in commands or search instructions to stand for a range of objects or characters.

Index

A

Abstract class, 155, 166
Access modifier, 136
Application programming
          interface (API), 6, 209
Argument, 40, 100, 104,
          110, 119, 209
ArrayList<Object>, 46
Assertion, 109–111, 185

B

Black-box testing, 173, 209
Bug(s)
    chaos, 193
    code-coverage, 175
    error handling, 107, 121
    execution of program, 17
    eyes, 39
    hypothesis, 200
    if statements, 65
    loop counter, 70
    OrderChecker/BankConnection, 182
    print statements, 190
    responsible, 199
    testing, 171

C

Call-by-value, 104
Checked exceptions, 112

Classes
    data, 142, 146, 148
    deep inheritance hierarchies, 177
    concrete, 155–156, 159, 163, 166
    CustomerAccount, 48
    error codes, 117
    equivalence, 173–175
    exception, 119
    god classes, 148–149
    Java, 196
    HistoryBoard, 42
    launching rocket, 141
    LeaderBoard, 42
    Main, 10, 11, 197
    members, 136, 144
    Order, 181–183
    partial view of, 37
    Product, 132, 137–139
    Scanner, 67
    scores, 41
    Shapes, 38, 40
    Shop, 139
    strategy, 193
    subroutines, 88, 98, 100
    testing, 178, 181, 184, 187
    utility, 149–150
    vehicle-registration program, 133
Cluttered code
    dead stuff, 16–17
    disabled stuff, 17
    unused stuff, 16

213

© Karl Beecher 2018
K. Beecher, *Bad Programming Practices 101*, https://doi.org/10.1007/978-1-4842-3411-2

Get the eBook for only $5!

Why limit yourself?

With most of our titles available in both PDF and ePUB format, you can access your content wherever and however you wish—on your PC, phone, tablet, or reader.

Since you've purchased this print book, we are happy to offer you the eBook for just $5.

To learn more, go to http://www.apress.com/companion or contact support@apress.com.

Apress®